Teach® Yourself

Get Your Articles Published

Lesley Bown and
Ann Gawthorpe

For UK order enquiries: please contact Bookpoint Ltd,
130 Milton Park, Abingdon, Oxon OX14 4SB.
Telephone: +44 (0) 1235 827720. Fax: +44 (0) 1235 400454.
Lines are open 09.00–17.00, Monday to Saturday, with a 24-hour
message answering service. Details about our titles and how to
order are available at www.teachyourself.com

For USA order enquiries: please contact McGraw-Hill
Customer Services, PO Box 545, Blacklick, OH 43004-0545,
USA. Telephone: 1-800-722-4726. Fax: 1-614-755-5645.

For Canada order enquiries: please contact McGraw-Hill
Ryerson Ltd, 300 Water St, Whitby, Ontario L1N 9B6,
Canada. Telephone: 905 430 5000. Fax: 905 430 5020.

Long renowned as the authoritative source for self-guided
learning – with more than 50 million copies sold worldwide –
the **Teach Yourself** series includes over 500 titles in the fields of
languages, crafts, hobbies, business, computing and education.

British Library Cataloguing in Publication Data: a catalogue record
for this title is available from the British Library.

Library of Congress Catalog Card Number: on file.

First published in UK 2008 by Hodder Education, part of
Hachette UK, 338 Euston Road, London NW1 3BH.

First published in US 2010 by The McGraw-Hill Companies, Inc.

Previously published as *Teach Yourself Writing for Magazines.*

The **Teach Yourself** name is a registered trade mark of
Hodder Headline.

Typeset by MPS, a Macmillan Company.

Printed in Great Britain for Hodder Education, an Hachette UK
Company, 338 Euston Road, London NW1 3BH, by CPI Cox &
Wyman, Reading, Berkshire RG1 8EX.

The publisher has used its best endeavours to ensure that the URLs
for external websites referred to in this book are correct and active
at the time of going to press. However, the publisher and the
author have no responsibility for the websites and can make no
guarantee that a site will remain live or that the content will remain
relevant, decent or appropriate.

Hachette UK's policy is to use papers that are natural, renewable
and recyclable products and made from wood grown in sustainable
forests. The logging and manufacturing processes are expected to
conform to the environmental regulations of the country of origin.

Impression number   10 9 8 7 6 5 4 3 2 1
Year   2014 2013 2012 2011 2010

Lesley and Ann dedicate this book to Mike and John.

Acknowledgements

Lesley and Ann are very grateful to everyone who helped with this book, and in particular Jan Barwick, Claire and Bob Bowen, Katy Bravery, Steve Egginton, Sarah Ford, Mary Frances, Gill Hudson, Mike and Jane Jago, Chris Jones, Elsbeth Lindner, Tim Rumball, Suzanne Ruthven, Tony Staveacre and Helen Tovey.

We would also like to thank *Horse + Pony*, *Motorcaravan Motorhome Monthly* and the *Weston Mercury* for allowing us to use examples from their pages.

Image credits

Front cover: © Digifoto Delta/Alamy

Back cover: © Jakub Semeniuk/iStockphoto.com, © Royalty-Free/Corbis, © agencyby/iStockphoto.com, © Andy Cook/iStockphoto.com, © Christopher Ewing/iStockphoto.com, © zebicho – Fotolia.com, © Geoffrey Holman/iStockphoto.com, © Photodisc/Getty Images, © James C. Pruitt/iStockphoto.com, © Mohamed Saber – Fotolia.com

Contents

Meet the authors

Welcome to *Get Your Articles Published*!

Neither of us intended to be journalists. Lesley wanted to write novels, while Ann had a passion for farce. And yet once you start writing it becomes a compulsion, and we each found ourselves looking round for other outlets for our work. Ann ended up working for a local paper, and then running her own magazine. Lesley went down the freelance route, writing humorous pieces for various publications as well as book reviews.

On the other hand, some of the people we spoke to in the course of researching this book were journalists first and foremost, with a passion for the craft of feature writing.

Whichever category you fall into, if you are starting out as a magazine writer you will find our book useful. We've included all our own favourite tips and hints, along with those shared with us by industry professionals. If you follow them, you will greatly increase your chances of getting published. Remember, an article means nothing until an editor uses it.

Lesley Bown and Ann Gawthorpe

Only got a minute?

▶ Start by writing about what you know such as your work, hobbies, or any other special expertise or personal experiences.

▶ Research the magazine market so that you don't send proposals to the wrong magazine. Get at least three recent issues and analyse their house style. Phone for the name of the person you should send your proposal to. Then send a query letter with a summary of your article, its length, whether you can provide photos and why you think it is suitable for the magazine.

▶ Write using short words, positive statements and active verbs. Make your opening paragraph short, snappy and intriguing. Your closing paragraph must follow naturally from the main part of the article. The rest of the paragraphs should flow logically.

▶ Leave it for a few days then rewrite to give it a final polish. Do a spellcheck, double-check facts and figures and make sure everyone's name is spelled correctly.

Type it on A4 paper, following the magazine's guidelines. Otherwise create a front cover with the article's title, your name, contact details, word count, number of pages and details of any illustrations. Also put your contact details and word count at the end of the article, in case it becomes separated from the cover page.

▶ Create a separate sheet for photos with their details and captions. Never write on the back of printed ones, although you can stick labels on them with your name, address and an identifying number.

5 Only got five minutes?

Getting started

Write about what you know such as your work, your hobby, or any other special expertise or personal experiences.

As editors will also want to see proof of your writing skills, build up a cuttings collection by writing without payment in club or school newsletters, church or local magazines, and so on.

Research the market

One of the most frequent complaints from editors is that they are sent ideas – and sometimes even fully written articles – which are completely unsuitable for their magazine. Obtain at least three recent issues of your chosen magazine and analyse them to ensure your article fits their requirements. Also obtain the magazine's writers' guidelines by looking online or phoning for them.

Make the initial approach by phone. Ask for the name of the person you should send your proposal to, and double-check the spelling of their name.

If they want a proposal, send a query letter with a summary of your article, its length, why you think it is suitable for their magazine, and what specific qualifications you have for writing it. Include your CV and copies of cuttings from your portfolio.

Writing

Choose a title for your article as it will help you stay focused on what exactly you are trying to do – but remember this might not be the final title.

Decide which pieces of information you want to use and then decide on their order, for example: chronological, building to a dramatic conclusion, or detailing the problem followed by its solution.

Write your article using short words, positive statements and active verbs. Make your opening paragraph short, snappy and intriguing. Your closing paragraph, which is equally important, must follow naturally from the main part of the article. Never 'tack on' an ending. The rest of the article should flow smoothly, with one paragraph following logically on from the previous one.

Quotations from interviews can be either direct speech in quotation marks or indirect speech preceded by 'that'.

When you have finished, leave your article for a few days and then write the second draft to give it a final polish. Spellcheck your writing, double-check facts and figures, and make sure everyone's name is spelled correctly. Check it for length and make any necessary alterations.

Presentation

Many magazines take emailed copy, but for hard copy use good quality A4 paper, and follow the magazine's guidelines on layout. If there aren't any guidelines, create a front cover with the article's title, your name, the word count, number of pages, details of any illustrations and your contact details.

Use wide margins all round, double-spaced text, and a double space between paragraphs. Don't allow paragraphs to run across from one page to the next. Number the pages and show how many there are altogether, for example 'page 1 of 8'. Put the article's title at the top of each page. At the bottom right of each page write 'more' or 'mf' (meaning 'more follows'), except the last which should finish with 'ends'. After 'ends', include your contact details and word count again, in case the article becomes separated from the cover page. Don't staple the pages together – if necessary use a paper clip.

Many magazines won't take articles without photos or illustrations. Create a separate sheet detailing the captions for them. Never write on the back of them, but do attach sticky labels on the rear, with your name, address and their identifying numbers.

Include a brief covering letter with the following information: the title of article, your name and a short reference to your brief.

Finally, before you post it off, make sure you have a copy of your article – either on the computer or a hard copy.

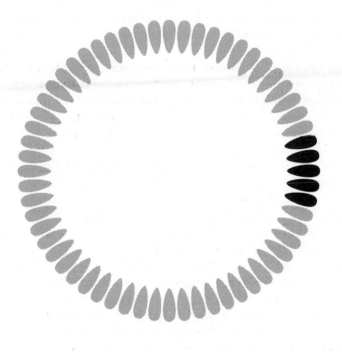

10 Only got ten minutes?

Getting started

Firstly, no magazines will take handwritten articles, so you will need a typewriter and preferably a computer.

Editors will want to see proof of your writing skills so build up a cuttings collection by writing without payment in club or school newsletters, church or local magazines, and so on.

Start by writing about what you know such as your work, your hobbies, or other special expertise or personal experiences. Other ideas can be triggered by news stories, press releases or browsing the internet.

Researching the market

To avoid rejection, research the magazine market – one of the most frequent complaints from editors is that they are sent ideas, and sometimes even fully written articles, which are completely unsuitable for their magazine.

Obtain at least three recent issues of a suitable magazine and analyse them. Is the writing style chatty or highbrow? Are topics covered in-depth, lightly or humorously? Request writers' guidelines by looking online or phoning for them.

Make the initial approach by phone. Ask for the name of the person you should send your proposal to, and double-check the spelling of the name. A letter starting 'Dear Sir or Madam' is just asking to be binned.

If they want a proposal, send a query letter with a summary of your article, its length, whether you can provide illustrations, why you think it is suitable for their magazine, and what specific qualifications you have for writing it. Include with it your CV and copies of cuttings from your portfolio.

If your proposal is accepted, check what the deadline for delivery is, whether it should be posted or emailed and what illustrations are wanted.

Making it saleable

Once you have an idea, make it attractive to the editor, by finding a new angle for it. For example, if you decide to write about stately homes, you could focus on those which have been used as films sets or for television series, or use a well-known format such as 'Top Ten stately homes'.

Or slant the article to appeal to specific magazines. For example, again using the example stately homes, you could concentrate on their gardens for gardening magazines or their kitchens for household and cookery magazines.

Research

Most articles need some research, even if it only involves checking statistics. There are many tools to help you research your ideas, including the internet, libraries, national newspapers, cuttings agencies and press offices. The internet is probably your first port of call but be aware that information has been uploaded by all kinds of people and may not always be accurate and reliable.

Interviews

Some articles will benefit from the inclusion of interviews. These can be done on the phone, by email or face to face. They can be brief to get some background information or a quote, or they can be an in-depth questioning.

Setting up the interview is the first point of contact between you and your interviewee; be professional, be friendly, be clear why you are contacting them and don't waffle. For the interview itself, have your questions prepared in advance and write up your notes and your first impressions straight afterwards.

Writing

Once you are ready to write, choose a title as it will help you stay focused on what exactly you are trying to do – but remember this might not be the final title. There are several different ways of titling an article, including using a question, a quotation, a pun or alliteration; which one you use will depend to a large extent on the type of magazine.

Decide which pieces of information you want to use and then decide on their order, for example: chronological, building to a dramatic conclusion, or detailing the problem followed by its solution.

Your opening paragraph, which sets the tone for the rest of the article, must grab the editor's attention. It can be a surprising opening statement, an anecdote or a scene-setting description. You can also use analogy, humour, a personal remark or a quotation. Keep the paragraph short, especially the first sentence and don't use anything which needs explaining such as jargon, foreign words, unusual abbreviations or complicated statistics.

Your closing paragraph is equally important and must follow quite naturally from the rest of the article. Never 'tack on' an ending. Different types of ending include a summary, a surprise, advice or a statement.

Between these two paragraphs the rest of the article should flow smoothly, with one paragraph following logically on from the previous one. Use bridging paragraphs to connect the first paragraph with the main body. These can be a nub paragraph which explains what the article is going to be about; a background information paragraph, which might contains facts and figures relevant to the piece; or a context paragraph which explains the circumstances surrounding the main thrust of the article.

Quotations from interviews can be displayed as direct speech in quotation marks or indirect speech preceded by 'said that'. Use direct quotes if they are short, pithy, contentious, emotional or explain a situation clearly. Other material from the interview can be compressed into indirect speech.

Use short words, positive statements and active verbs for example 'the cat sat on the mat' rather than 'the mat was sat on by the cat'. Avoid specialist vocabulary, clichés and empty words.

When you have finished, leave your article for a few days and then write the second draft to give it a final polish. Spellcheck your writing, double-check facts and figures and make sure everyone's name is spelled correctly. Check the article for length and make any necessary alterations.

Illustrating it

Many magazines won't accept articles unless you can also provide photographs as well. If you have reasonable expertise with a camera, take the photos yourself. Otherwise use a professional freelance photographer or pay for photos from picture libraries or agencies.

Presentation

Many magazines take emailed copy but for hard copy use good quality A4 paper, and follow the magazine's guidelines on layout. If there aren't any, create a front cover with the article's title, your name, the word count, number of pages, details of any illustrations and your contact details.

Use wide margins all round, double-spaced text, and a double space between paragraphs. Don't allow paragraphs to run across from one page to the next. Number the pages and show how many there are altogether, for example 'page 1 of 8'. Put the article's title at the top of each page. At the bottom right of each page put 'more' or 'mf' (meaning 'more follows'), except the last which should finish with 'ends'. After 'ends' write your contact details and the word count again, in case the article becomes separated from the cover page. Don't staple the pages together – if necessary use a paper clip.

If there are photos or illustrations, create a separate sheet detailing the captions for them. Never write on the back of them, but do attach sticky labels on the rear with your name, address and their identifying numbers.

Include a brief covering letter with the following information: the title of article, your name and a short reference to the brief.

Finally, before you post it off make sure you have a copy of your article, either on the computer or a hard copy.

Introduction

Can anyone be a journalist? Yes.

Can anyone be a successful journalist? That will depend on talent, hard work and luck.

We are living in the information age. There is more information available than any of us can absorb, and most of us have less time to spend acquiring information than ever before. That is where magazines come in. We rely on journalists to select and interpret information, and present it to us in an accessible form. Whether it's a round-up of the new season's fashion or an in-depth analysis of global warming, we can find the information we need in the relevant magazine.

As a result there is a vast range of magazines available today. The average high street newsagent will stock between 500 and 1,000 (depending on the time of year) and larger branches of WH Smith will have as many as 2,000. Add to this all the free magazines, the trade magazines, the magazines that various organizations send to their members, and you can see there is a never-ending need for written material.

What's more, most magazines are under-staffed. Staff writers work at a frantic pace trying to keep up with their deadlines, and as a result almost all magazines carry contributions from freelance writers.

Despite this, however, it can be very difficult for the freelance writer to find a way into the world of writing for magazines. This book aims to help you avoid the common mistakes of the novice writer and to show you how to produce articles that are both publishable and saleable.

Why write?

Of course not all readers of this book will be interested in the money side of writing for magazines. People write for all sorts of reasons:

- ▶ *as a one-off*
- ▶ *as a hobby*
- ▶ *for a second income*
- ▶ *as a career.*

ONE-OFF

So why do you want to write articles? You might want to write just one article, to express a point of view on something you feel strongly about, or you may have been asked to write a piece* because of your particular expertise.

HOBBY

You may see article writing as a hobby to be fitted in around full-time employment, raising a family or enjoying retirement.

SECOND INCOME

Writing articles can produce a steady stream of income to bolster your finances.

CAREER

If you want to make writing for magazines your full-time career, see Chapters 26 and 27.

Whatever your motivation, the basics will be the same – you will need to write clearly, accurately and in a way that keeps your readers interested. You will need to do research, keep records and liaise with your editor or editors. These skills are common

*Piece: article

to all magazine writing, and without them you are unlikely to be successful.

This book takes you through all the stages of writing, researching and submitting a magazine article. There are examples throughout the book and exercises to help you, and we also analyse two of our own articles. Journalistic vocabulary is explained as we go along in the footnotes, with a summary of all the jargon at the end of the book. Also at the end of the book you will find sample writers' guidelines, a list of useful websites and a booklist.

Everyone should read the section on Income Tax in Chapter 27, since all earnings from writing are taxable, even if it is just a hobby.

Qualities needed

If you have an interest in words and how they are strung together, you can learn the writing skills needed to get your articles published – but of course there is more to it than just being a competent writer. You will also need other qualities as well. These include:

- *confidence in your own abilities*
- *an ability to generate ideas*
- *a willingness to produce what editors want*
- *an ability to meet deadlines*
- *curiosity*
- *perseverance*
- *people skills*
- *networking skills*
- *an ability to cope with rejection*
- *an ability to cope with insecurity.*

CONFIDENCE IN YOUR OWN ABILITIES

To be a freelance writer you have to be proactive. Unless you are a household name, or top in your field of expertise, it is unlikely that editors are going to beat a path to your door begging you to write for them. Following the advice in this book should give you the confidence to approach editors knowing that you have saleable material to offer them.

AN ABILITY TO GENERATE IDEAS

Most literate people could, if they set their mind to it, learn to write competent copy* – and certainly all magazines have staff writers who can do that. The core problem for almost all publications is the need to come up with a continual flow of ideas, and if you can generate ideas for articles then you are more than halfway to success. In Chapter 5 we give advice on how to come up with new ideas and how to make one idea go a long way.

A WILLINGNESS TO PRODUCE WHAT EDITORS WANT

Editors have to keep an eye on two interrelated factors – what their readers want to read, and what their advertisers want from the magazine. Once you have your ideas, then it is necessary to find the right magazine for them. You are just asking for rejection if you send ideas which don't meet a particular magazine's requirements. In Chapter 4 we go into more detail on analysing magazines and assessing their requirements.

AN ABILITY TO MEET DEADLINES

Both magazines and newspapers are driven by their deadlines. A writer who is consistently late with work will never be successful, and even sending work in at the last possible minute will make you unpopular.

CURIOSITY

Journalists are always asking questions, and good journalists ask the questions their readers are interested in having answered.

*copy: written material, the words that make up the article

If a writer isn't curious about a subject and therefore interested in finding out more about it, it is unlikely a magazine editor will be enthused about it either.

PERSEVERANCE

This important quality goes without saying, especially at the beginning when you are trying to establish a reputation. If one magazine is not interested in your ideas – try another one. Always have several ideas or articles out there in the marketplace and constantly keep adding to your list of ideas to investigate for future articles.

PEOPLE SKILLS

Journalists need to be good listeners, with an ability to get people to relax and open up to them.

NETWORKING SKILLS

Journalists need contacts – people to interview, people to provide background information, people to help with research.

AN ABILITY TO COPE WITH REJECTION

Rejections are inevitable. It may be that the magazine has already featured that particular idea, or that it was wrong for their readership, or that it just didn't enthuse the editor. They are not rejecting you as a person, so don't take it personally. If you think the idea still has potential, find another market immediately.

AN ABILITY TO COPE WITH INSECURITY

The nature of freelance journalism means that there is little routine and little that is predictable about the work. And anyone trying to make a living as a freelancer will have to be able to cope with financial insecurity.

Libel and legal queries

Writers have to take into account that there are laws relating to what they can write about, particularly the law of libel. While most journalists won't be writing features which might be open to litigation, it has to be borne in mind. You should keep all notes relating to an article and records of interviews in case of query by the sub editor or the magazine's legal department.

Because this is a specialist area, outside the scope of this book, writers should take professional advice and consult a lawyer or the many excellent books on law. It is sometimes possible for journalists to take out insurance against libel and other legal problems, and for this you would need to consult a specialist broker.

Using this book

The book is divided into four parts. Part one takes you through the process of researching the market, generating ideas, carrying out the research and submitting proposals. Part two shows you how to write a publishable article. Part three outlines the different options available to the writer and Part four expands on making writing a full-time business – including starting your own magazine.

We have included a feature called 'Work in progress' which shows the process of finding an idea, researching it and then writing it up. There are also exercises at the end of the chapters in Parts one, two and three, and plenty of examples throughout to clarify the points being made. Many of the examples are from our own published articles and are printed courtesy of *Horse + Pony* magazine, *Motorcaravan Motorhome Monthly* and the *Weston Mercury*, and others have been specially written to illustrate a point.

Although we have included a few websites in each chapter, there are plenty of useful sites, shown in chapter order, in Appendix B at the end of the book.

Remember, although it's demanding work, getting your articles published can be rewarding both intellectually and financially. It can give you the opportunity to meet many interesting people and to find out about a wide range of subjects.

Good luck!

Lesley and Ann

Part one
Getting started

1

....

Practical basics

In this chapter you will learn:
- *what equipment you need*
- *how to organize your time*
- *what skills you need.*

You'll need belief in yourself, an ability to cope with rejections (think of each rejection as one step closer to eventual acceptance), determination to succeed and stamina.

Jan Barwick, Editor, *Devon Life*

Before you start work give some thought to the basic practicalities:

▶ *equipment*
▶ *space*
▶ *working pattern*
▶ *skills*
▶ *software*
▶ *reference material.*

Equipment

It is possible to write for magazines with almost no equipment – a borrowed typewriter, a library ticket and some change for a phone box would just about get you started. However, if at all possible, you should have a computer and a phone of your own. Other equipment can be added as necessary.

COMPUTER

No matter how beautiful your handwriting, editors will not accept handwritten copy. Unless your article is going to be a one-off, invest in a computer. This makes it easy for you to store information, make alterations to your articles and print off immaculate copies. Most have facilities for cutting CDs or DVDs and if your article is to be illustrated with your own photographs, many editors prefer the pictures to be sent on CDs rather than having to download them from an email.

Insight

A laptop – as well as or instead of a PC – is useful for taking to interviews and libraries and so on, as you can then write up notes straight away. Be sure to have the battery fully charged.

INTERNET ACCESS

Internet access is invaluable for researching online and also allows you to email copy directly to the editor. However, check first that this is acceptable to them, since some still prefer articles to be sent by post. A broadband connection will also speed up internet access and make it easier for surfing the internet.

CAMERA

A camera should preferably be digital with a high pixel* number – at least 8 mega pixels (see Chapter 18).

TAPE RECORDER

A tape recorder or voice recorder is useful for interviews, even though you may also take notes at the same time.

*pixel: short for 'picture element'. Pictures are made up from thousands of dots of colour. As a rule of thumb the more pixels there are to the inch the better the quality of the picture.

Space

As well as enough space for your typewriter or computer, you will need somewhere to keep your paperwork; the paperless office has yet to materialize and even the most dedicated user of electronic media will find they accumulate press releases, books, pamphlets and pages of notes from research or interviews. However big or small your space, try to organize it efficiently and you will get much more work done.

Working pattern

Unless you plan to be a very occasional writer, you will need to be disciplined in establishing a work routine. Most freelance writers are not full-timers, and fit their writing in around their main job or childcare commitments. Try to establish regular routines and times when you will be at your desk, come what may.

Insight

Your mind doesn't work to a rigid timetable and once you are in the habit of writing you will find that new ideas and answers to current writing problems come to you at all sorts of odd times, so always carry a notebook.

Skills

KEYBOARD

The faster you are on the keyboard, the easier you will find it to produce copy and it is worth taking a little time to master ten-finger typing ('touch typing'). If you struggle with typing, then perhaps voice recognition software would help.

Shorthand takes a while to learn and many journalists manage without it, but if you plan to do a lot of interviewing then it is worth considering. Teeline and T-script are systems which rely on word abbreviations and are considered easier to learn than the traditional Pitman's shorthand (see Appendix B).

Software

Most computers come loaded with programs which allow you to write articles and print them off. It is also possible to buy specialist software which can be useful for managing large amounts of information produced by research, and for record keeping (see Appendix B).

Reference material

Although computers generally come with a spellchecker, a good dictionary is still important. It is also worth investing in a thesaurus to give you a range of words with similar meanings and a book on grammar to check on aspects you are unsure of. Alternatively, use the internet for this information if you prefer.

Other reference books will depend on the type of articles you propose writing. To keep costs down, it is worthwhile checking for second-hand copies of them on www.amazon.co.uk or www.amazon.com.

Another useful source for building up your reference library is charity shops, which carry all kinds of interesting books which can be bought for a few pounds. Aim to acquire some basic books of general knowledge, as well as books relating to your specialist subjects.

If you prefer to use websites, remember that not all of them contain reliable information (see Appendix B).

Mary Frances

I'd been writing since I was old enough to hold a pencil but was obliged to work at boring cash-on-a-Friday jobs. Finally, I decided to qualify for something where I could use my writing skills and earn money at the same time, and at the age of 70 went back to college. Within three months I had broken my elbow, developed arthritis in both hips, lost my current job and run out of money. So I applied for housing benefit. The result was bizarre and chaotic. Having to write an assignment for college, I described these wonderful tussles, decided they should reach a wider audience and sent them as a feature to the local paper – which promptly gave me a job. Despite elbow, hips and cash flow, the journalism course was completed, with several distinctions, and an award – National Senior Learner of the Year for 2002.

10 THINGS TO REMEMBER

1　*You can start writing with a typewriter, but aim to acquire a computer plus printer.*

2　*Access to a phone is all-important.*

3　*Access to the internet (preferably with a broadband connection) is useful for research.*

4　*Keep a notebook to hand for recording ideas and information, which may come to you when you're least expecting it!*

5　*Be realistic about the time you have available for writing.*

6　*Learn ten-finger typing ('touch typing').*

7　*Shorthand is a useful skill, but not essential.*

8　*It's important to organize a dedicated space for writing.*

9　*Buy a dictionary and thesaurus.*

10　*Collect reference books; second-hand ones will do.*

2

Making a start

In this chapter you will learn:
- *about the importance of building a portfolio*
- *how to practise your skills*
- *where to start.*

> *It you want to be a writer, start simply. Keep a journal. You can't be a writer without being an observer.*
>
> Jan Barwick, Editor, *Devon Life*

Even if your ultimate aim is to be paid for what you write, you may need to do some unpaid work first. You will need to:

- ▶ *build up your portfolio*
- ▶ *practise your skills.*

Building up your portfolio

Editors like to see a portfolio of a writer's previous work if they are being asked to commission an article on the basis of a proposal*. They need some reassurance that you have the skills and stamina to carry out what you propose. Some of the pieces that you write for free will be good enough to go in your portfolio.

*proposal: suggestion for an article

Practising your skills

You may like the idea of writing articles, but unless you already work in journalism you won't know if you can master the type of writing required. Writing reports in a commercial environment, or academic essays, or letters to friends, are all quite different from feature* writing.

All of the media discussed below provide opportunities for you to try your hand at writing for publication. However, many of them will not apply professional standards to your work. Some of them may be so desperate for material they will take almost anything, others will be more selective – but don't assume that success in any of these areas means you are good enough to be paid for your writing.

You can still learn a lot from the experience. If you found the work tedious – and kept putting off having to sit down and write – then you probably aren't cut out to be a magazine writer. Also you will learn how different your work looks in print. Wait until the initial excitement of seeing it in print has worn off and look through your piece objectively. In particular, look for anything that was changed from your original. Ask yourself why the editor needed to do that.

The best of your successes can be included in your portfolio (see Chapter 6). Editors will recognize that you weren't paid for the material, but at least they will be able to see that you can write.

There are innumerable opportunities to practise your writing skills as long as you don't want to be paid. These include:

- ▶ *local newsletters*
- ▶ *local newspapers*
- ▶ *parish magazines*

*feature: another word for an article; includes everything the reader will see on the page, such as pictures or tables.

- ▶ *company magazines*
- ▶ *membership magazines*
- ▶ *college/university newsletters*
- ▶ *fanzines*
- ▶ *e-zines*
- ▶ *press releases.*

LOCAL NEWSLETTERS

Small local organizations and clubs usually produce a newsletter. They can be anything from a printed booklet to photocopied pages and are increasingly sent as emails. The editor is nearly always short of material and grateful for anything that is sent in. If you belong to a badminton club, a drama group or any other local group, offer to write about something relevant, or to report an event.

LOCAL NEWSPAPERS

Consider becoming a correspondent for your local newspaper. This involves collecting information from local clubs, groups and organizations and putting them together in one report. You may even be paid 'lineage' – which is a set amount for each line printed in the paper – or per word.

There is always a chance that you will come across an interesting story which can be written up as a news story and will be published in the main part of the paper. You will still be paid lineage and it can be added to your portfolio. Even better, it might carry your byline*.

PARISH MAGAZINES

Like newsletters, these are usually small black and white publications, often produced by just one person. Many are not confined to church-goers and carry reports on the life of the parish.

*byline: a reporter's name on an article

COMPANY MAGAZINES

Big companies often produce magazines that are circulated to the employees. They are usually professionally produced, either in-house* by the PR department or by an outside specialist company. However, if you are an employee you have a very good chance of having your piece accepted.

MEMBERSHIP MAGAZINES

Most large membership organizations produce a high quality glossy magazine for their members. Again, these are often professionally produced but there may be openings for members to submit material. Occasionally the material is entirely provided by members.

COLLEGE/UNIVERSITY NEWSLETTERS

These are usually professionally produced and sent to the alumni of the college or university. There are openings for alumni who have an interesting story to tell, to send in contributions.

FANZINES

As the name suggests, these are small publications written by (and for) fans of a particular interest, such as sport or music, or a celebrity. Often promoting a narrow viewpoint, they are usually written, edited and published by one person on a not-for-profit basis. They can be found in both paper and internet form.

E-ZINES

Sometimes called electronic magazines, these can be both the internet version of an existing magazine or magazines which exist only on the internet. See Chapter 3 for further information.

*in-house: work that is done within a company rather than being sent to outside specialists

PRESS RELEASES

A good source of writing practise is to offer to write press releases for any small club or group that you are a member of. They won't be able to pay you, but they will need someone to tell the local paper about their forthcoming events, fundraising and so on. This is a good way to get yourself known to editors of the local press.

Money earning opportunities

READERS' DIGEST

This was a useful outlet for short, humorous stories, but at the time of writing its future is uncertain.

LETTERS

Another good practice area for beginners is the letters page that virtually all magazines have. Many of these pay for the letters, and usually there is an extra payment for one selected letter. It is possible to earn £50 or more for less than 200 words with a well-written letter.

If you plan to write a lot of letters then keep copies to avoid duplication. Don't send the same letter to several publications (although if you are campaigning for something that is important to you, you can fire off a series of similar letters).

Humour is welcome on letters pages, so keep a record of amusing incidents that happen to you, your friends and your family and learn to write them up in an economical but amusing way.

Insight
Don't include letters in your portfolio, and you mustn't list the publications that take your letters as if they had bought articles from you.

Sarah Ford, staff writer, *Somerset Life*

My route into writing for magazines was quite a conventional one. After taking a degree in English and Media I went to work for a local newspaper to get on-the-job training. During that time I did a ten-week NCTJ course in Sheffield.

After gaining my NCTJ* qualification I went to work in local radio and then public relations. I then returned to a local newspaper where I was a news editor before becoming a writer for *Somerset Life* magazine. The switch from writing for newspapers to writing for magazines is not as great as first seems because local reporters have to write articles as well as news stories.

Exercises
- ▶ *Compile a list of newsletters and so on that you receive and write something for at least one of them.*
- ▶ *Choose a topic for a letter and write it as if you were going to send it to different magazines, changing the style to suit the magazine.*

*NCTJ: National Council for the Training of Journalists.

10 THINGS TO REMEMBER

1 *Editors like to see a portfolio of work.*

2 *Feature writing is a special skill.*

3 *Unpaid work is good practice.*

4 *Start by contacting the publications you already receive and are familiar with.*

5 *Check out e-zines on the internet.*

6 *Contact your local newspaper and offer to act as a correspondent.*

7 *Letters pages often pay quite well.*

8 *Humour is often welcome on letters pages.*

9 *Don't include letters as examples in your portfolio.*

10 *Offer to do the publicity for local groups – you will get to know editors of the local press.*

3

Understanding the market

In this chapter you will learn:
- *how the magazine business works*
- *about different types of magazines*
- *about magazine content.*

Good magazines target their audiences, and don't look favourably on a piece that has been touted around to lots of other magazines. One size does NOT fit all. You should always ask: why this, why now, and why for this particular magazine?

Gill Hudson, former Editor, *Radio Times*

There are thousands of periodicals in the UK. Roughly one-third of these are consumer magazines and the remainder trade, professional or academic publications. So, even though you may have a brilliant idea that you are itching to write, you should first of all spend time analysing the market to see which would be the best option for your piece.

One of the most frequent complaints from editors is that they are sent ideas and sometimes even fully-written articles which are completely unsuitable for their magazine. This not only results in rejection, but when you do have an idea which is suitable for them, they may not want to know.

The magazine business

Most magazines are obliged to make a profit, but some are run as a service to members, or for some other reason that means they only have to cover their costs. Whatever the level of profit required, the economics of magazine production means this can't be achieved by the cover charge* but is dependent on advertising revenue or brand extension*.

Consumer magazines get a large percentage – more than half – of their income from advertising and the rest from the cover charge. Most of these magazines will have between 30 per cent and 50 per cent of the space taken up with advertising although some have more than this. Trade magazines tend to have a higher percentage of advertising and less editorial content.

Distribution costs for magazines are high and for this reason publishers encourage subscriptions by offering substantial reductions on the cover charge.

Advertising rates are based on the magazine's success. Success is measured in various ways including:

▶ **circulation:** *the number of copies sold*
▶ **readership:** *the number of readers, which will be more than one per copy sold*
▶ **penetration:** *the percentage of the target market that buys a magazine.*

*cover charge: the price paid by the reader

*brand extension: selling to the readership under the magazine's name items such as furniture and holidays

Types of publication

Within each genre there could be a dozen or more titles, which come out weekly, monthly, bi-monthly, quarterly or annually. While it will depend on the size and type of the magazine, generally speaking weekly titles will need more articles overall than monthly ones and therefore will offer more scope for the freelance writer.

Publications can be divided into five main groups:

- *general consumer*
- *dedicated consumer*
- *newspapers*
- *specialist*
- *e-zines and fanzines.*

GENERAL CONSUMER

These include:

- *women's (e.g.* Women and Home, She*)*
- *men's (e.g.* GQ, Loaded*)*
- *children and teenagers (e.g. the* Beano, Mizz*)*
- *parenting (e.g.* Mother and Baby*)*
- *lifestyle (e.g.* Saga Magazine*)*
- *gossip and celebrity (e.g.* Heat, OK*)*
- *modern culture (e.g.* New Statesman, Contemporary Review*).*

DEDICATED CONSUMER

These include:

- *hobbyist (e.g.* Leisure Painter, Motor Cycle News*)*
- *sport (e.g.* Cycle Sport, Angling Times*)*
- *homes and household (e.g.* Ideal Home, Homes and Gardens*)*
- *airline (e.g.* easyJet Inflight *magazine)*
- *regional magazines (e.g.* Lincolnshire Life, Somerset Life*).*

NEWSPAPERS

These include:

▶ *national*
▶ *local*
▶ *newspaper supplements.*

Feature writing is different from news writing but if you look through most newspapers you will see that a lot of the content is features. News occupies the first few pages, but after that there will be articles on fashion, lifestyle, health and so on. These use a magazine-type format and offer scope for freelancers. Weekend editions of papers usually include a colour supplement which is also full of features.

SPECIALIST

These include:

▶ *trade and business-to-business (e.g.* Computer Weekly, Restaurant *magazine)*
▶ *technical (e.g.* Scientific Computing World, Engineering*)*
▶ *in-house (e.g.* Accumulate, *a magazine sent to customers of Standard Life).*

In-house magazines are published by companies either for their employees or for their customers. They can in fact be outsourced to specialist production companies but they are still known as in-house magazines.

E-ZINES AND FANZINES

E-zines, which exist only on the internet and do not have a traditional paper version, are still in their infancy. So far they include mainly American sites such as:

▶ *Helium.com which allows writers to upload articles on a range of topics. There are also opportunities to write for specific companies on specific topics and to evaluate the merits of other writers' articles. It is possible to be paid for articles and the site also runs competitions with cash prizes.*

▶ *BellaOnline.com which is for women writers only. There is no money on offer, but it invites writers to become editors with regular slots on the site.*

Fanzines are us ually looking for articles from highly knowledgeable writers in their specialist area.

> **Insight**
> E-zines and fanzines are usually non-profit making, and so don't pay for copy. They can provide a good source of practice however, and can help to build up your portfolio.

Magazine content

Mainstream magazine content tends to follow conventional lines. Consumer magazines will usually include fiction, readers' letters, horoscopes, listings, reviews, crosswords and other puzzles, regular columns and the editor's column as well as features. Other types of magazine are more likely to be restricted to articles around the subject of the magazine – you wouldn't expect to find horoscopes in a technical magazine or fiction in a business magazine.

Types of article

The different types of articles could include:

▶ *news*
▶ *news background*
▶ *profiles and interviews*

- *features*
- *regular columns*
- *personal accounts*
- *humour*
- *how-to*
- *fiction*
- *puzzles/quizzes.*

NEWS

In the main, this will be soft news rather than the hard news headlined in the newspapers. It can include product news and reports on recent events.

NEWS BACKGROUND

These are articles which explore recent events in depth. They may be slanted towards the particular magazine in which they appear.

PROFILES AND INTERVIEWS

How famous the interviewee has to be will depend on the type of magazine. Upmarket and high circulation magazines will be interested in interviews with well-known people such as politicians and celebrities. Local and regional magazines are more likely to run interviews with local people who are in some way unusual or noteworthy. Specialist magazines run interviews with people who are well known in their field but unknown outside of it.

FEATURES

These form the meat of the magazine and are enormously wide ranging – anything from famous houses to a collection of doormats. Generally speaking they provide the biggest opportunity for freelancers because staff writers often don't have the time to do the necessary research.

REGULAR COLUMNS

These are the regular items which appear in every issue covering topics such as health, gardening and legal matters. They include advice columns that answer readers' queries on a topic and are often written by freelancers.

PERSONAL ACCOUNTS

One way of starting is to write about yourself. If you have done anything interesting or out of the ordinary, or have undergone a life-changing or illuminating experience which you wish to share then write it down and turn it into an article. However, personal experiences don't have to be quite so dramatic to find an outlet – a small incident can be turned into a humorous feature.

The more emotive of these pieces are known as 'TOTs' or 'Triumph Over Tragedy' and are often written by a professional journalist who interviews the person concerned – but there is no reason why you shouldn't write your own story.

HUMOUR

Light-hearted articles are welcome in some magazines, but overall the market for humour is a small one.

HOW-TO

This lucrative genre includes recipes, gardening tips and giving practical advice on anything from grooming your dog to fitting a new bathroom. You need both the expertise and the ability to explain the task clearly (see Chapter 22).

FICTION

This is a very specific writing genre and dealt with in detail in Chapter 25.

PUZZLES/QUIZZES

This is a highly specialized field, but if you have the knack for devising puzzles it can be very rewarding. Bear in mind that you would need to keep up a constant flow.

Magazine personnel

The production of a magazine involves a number of people each with their specific roles. On smaller magazines, staff may have to take on more than one function while on the larger ones each section will have its own group of staff. Generally speaking the main roles and their functions are:

- ► **editor:** *responsible for the editorial content and style of the magazine. On smaller magazines he/she may also be responsible for generating feature ideas, writing articles and liaising with production staff.*
- ► **deputy editor:** *assists the editor and may be responsible for one or more sections.*
- ► **features editor:** *responsible for specialist features such as fashion, beauty and lifestyles. On large magazines each of these specialist sections will have their own editor.*
- ► **news editor:** *responsible for writing the news stories in magazines.*
- ► **sub editor (or sub):** *responsible for rewriting where necessary and checking copy for spelling, grammar and legal requirements. They also write the headings and layout the pages.*
- ► **copy editor:** *same as a sub editor (a title mainly used in America).*
- ► **production editor:** *responsible for managing schedules and ensuring the magazine is ready for publication on time.*
- ► **commissioning editor:** *only found on large magazines, responsible for commissioning articles, particularly from freelancers.*

- ▶ **picture editor:** *responsible for commissioning photos, organizing photo shoots, maintaining picture libraries and so on. Also responsible for managing digital images and editing.*
- ▶ **staff writer/reporter:** *employed by the magazine to provide copy.*

Elsbeth Lindner, Editor, *newbooks*

My path to journalism came via 30 years spent in book publishing. So, for many years, I worked on other people's writing and prose. After emigrating from the UK to the USA, I decided to stop being a publisher and try my hand at book reviewing. Despite a trend towards shrinking book pages in their newspapers, the US still offers many more places where reviews are published and I was fortunate to be offered try-outs by several newspapers. Simultaneously, I had maintained contact with a UK literary magazine called *newbooks* and from my US vantage post found myself invited to interview American writers for the UK-based magazine. This work has developed various lateral tentacles over the last few years and I have taken over as editor of *newbooks*. One of my decisions as Editor has been to commission fewer interviews from myself!

Exercises
- ▶ *Make a list of all the magazines, newsletters and so on, that you buy, subscribe to or receive for free.*
- ▶ *Make a list of all the magazines, newsletters and so on, that you regularly have sight of.*

10 THINGS TO REMEMBER

1   *Magazines target their readership.*

2   *Analyse the market before you start writing.*

3   *Do not annoy editors by sending them unsuitable ideas.*

4   *Understand magazine economics.*

5   *Most magazines need to make a profit, which usually comes from advertising.*

6   *Advertising rates depend on circulation.*

7   *There are many types of magazine, don't confine yourself to the most obvious ones.*

8   *Understand the many different types of magazine.*

9   *Writing features may provide the biggest opportunities for new writers.*

10   *Writing profiles may be a way of getting started.*

4

Researching magazines

In this chapter you will learn:
- *how to target a magazine*
- *about layout*
- *how to analyse a magazine.*

> *Beg, borrow or steal a few recent issues and analyse them.*
> *Study a) the writing style – the tone of voice that's used in*
> *the mag. Is it chirpy? Educated? Highbrow?*
> *Then b) look at the little slug lines at the top of each feature –*
> *like 'real people', 'health', 'comment', 'at home', etc. And*
> *don't suggest anything, really, that wouldn't fit in the next*
> *issue of the magazine in one of those slots.*
>
> Katy Bravery, Deputy Editor, Saga Magazine

Before writing anything, you need to know that there is a market
for your material. Some topics are so specialized that they will
only be saleable to a tiny number of publications. The technical
specifications of aircraft, or academic research into a minor
literary figure, are never going to reach a wide market. Most
topics, however, have a surprisingly wide range of possibilities
(see Chapter 5 for more on this).

Choosing a magazine

Most new writers turn to the general consumer magazines when
thinking of outlets for articles, but while some publications

are almost entirely written by freelancers, others use very little freelance material.

Insight

Check the magazine listings in the *Writers' Handbook*, the *Writers and Artists' Yearbook* or the *Writers' Market* (which also has a website www.writersmarket.co.uk). For the American market, use the USA version of *Writer's Market*.

Many magazines aren't listed in these publications and for those you will have to phone or email to find out what their editorial policy is. Several magazines which do take articles are included in Appendix B.

If you have an article in mind, start with those magazines that could be potential markets, otherwise start with a magazine that you enjoy reading yourself.

Insight

Don't start with one of the 'big sellers' as they are the most difficult magazines to break into. Look at smaller publications with lower circulations, such as local or specialist magazines.

If you have the required knowledge and expertise, there may be more opportunities in the dedicated consumer magazines or the specialist press described in Chapter 3. Although these magazines are not available on the newsagents' shelves, it is easy to track many of them down via the internet. Appendix B includes several large publishers' websites which list the magazines they publish.

Subscriber-only magazines are more difficult to track down, but they can be found on the internet. Pick a subject you are interested in, such as bird watching, then type into your search engine 'magazines about bird watching' and some websites will pop up.

Whichever magazine you decide to aim for, it is vital to analyse it in depth to ensure that your article matches the style of the magazine (see below for how to do this).

House style

Every publication has what is known as a 'house style'. This covers a range of practical aspects from whether to use double or single quotation marks, to the style of page layout used.

However you write your article it will be converted into the house style before going to print – but if you try to capture the house style of your chosen magazine, you stand a better chance of your article being chosen. If it is going to take too long to make the changes the editor may decide not to bother with your article, however interesting it is.

WRITERS' GUIDELINES

To find out more about the house style of any particular magazine contact them and ask for their writers' guidelines. Sometimes these can be downloaded from the magazine's website. Not all magazines produce writers' guidelines but most do. It will include information about the most important aspects of house style, type of feature required, length, whether illustrations and photographs are essential and how to submit an article or propose an idea. Sample guidelines are given in Appendix A.

Page furniture

Magazines rarely consist of solid blocks of text. Most features consist of the main copy combined with an arrangement of photographs, tables, information boxes and so on. Sometimes the information in them is provided by the writer of the main copy, but sometimes other people are commissioned to provide it. For example, an editor may decide that your piece about walking in the Lake District needs fleshing out with some statistics about the number of visitors to the Lakes and may ask a staffer* to dig them out. Or a piece about your experience of having a kidney transplant may be supplemented by some medical information provided by a doctor.

These features that support published articles are often known as 'extras' and there are several types:

- ▶ **box:** *for simple facts (make sure they are accurate)*
- ▶ **table:** *for complicated facts (make sure they are accurate)*
- ▶ **sidebar:** *a self-contained section alongside the main article*
- ▶ **paragraphs:** *for facts that need explanation (write short clear paragraphs for setting in boxes).*

In addition there are:

- ▶ **headlines:** *the title*
- ▶ **strap lines:** *these go above the headline and are usually provocative to catch the eye*
- ▶ **subheadings:** *these go below the headline and expand on it*
- ▶ **crossheads:** *small headings that break up the article*
- ▶ **standfirst:** *an introductory paragraph, often in larger type than the main text (they are usually written by the sub editor and will include the writer's byline)*
- ▶ **highlight quote:** *a sentence from the article in large print.*

*staffer: journalist employed as part of the permanent staff

Content

All publications also have a style related to content – the way topics are treated, whether lightly or in depth, and the kind of topics that are chosen.

The easiest way to achieve an understanding of this principal is to buy several newspapers on the same day and see how each one deals with the main story of the day. Magazines, of course, are less likely to deal with the same topic at the same time, (apart from the seasonal topics such as Christmas) but you will need to understand your chosen magazine's agenda and approach. You can compare how several magazines review the same film, or interview the same celebrity, to get an idea of different approaches to the same subject.

How to analyse a magazine

Before you set about writing something for the magazine, you need to understand exactly what makes the magazine work, and to achieve this you need to analyse the following aspects:

▶ *contents page*
▶ *news pages*
▶ *regular items*
▶ *readers' letters and emails*
▶ *other items*
▶ *adverts*
▶ *one-off features.*

CONTENTS PAGE

Most contents pages include information about the editorial team and how to contact them. Make a note of the names so that when you look at the features you can see which were written by staffers and which by freelancers. Also take note that for most magazines there are very few names – only the biggest have a large staff. The contents information will give you an idea of the magazine's balance between the various types of item.

NEWS PAGES

Magazines don't usually deal with hard news but there are often one or more pages of news round-up, where recent events relevant to the readership are highlighted. A magazine for cyclists might mention a new type of lightweight saddle, a record-breaking attempt to cycle around the world or a change in the law about cycle helmets. These pages are usually written by staffers and are largely compiled from press releases, but they give you valuable information about the tone of the magazine. Many of the items have the potential to be expanded into features in later issues.

REGULAR ITEMS

These are the magazine's bread and butter and many readers will turn to their favourite first – whether it's the editor's piece or the celebrity opinion piece (often placed at the end of the magazine). Apart from celebrity pieces, they are usually written either by staffers or by freelancers with a regular commission. In some magazines they will include one or more technical columns written by someone with expertise, possibly answering readers' queries.

READERS' LETTERS AND EMAILS

Reading the letters will tell you a lot about the readers and their concerns. Bear in mind that someone on the staff will have selected the best or most relevant letters, so their choices will also tell you how the editorial staff see their magazine's image. Some magazines also add readers' postings on their website.

OTHER ITEMS

Reviews, competitions, puzzles and marketing offers; they all add to the feel of the magazine and will help you understand its target readership.

This is a very important part of your analysis. Go through the magazine page by page and make a note of all the adverts. Advertisers are an independent source of understanding about the magazine's readership, since they have to decide where best to spend their money (and full-colour, glossy ads are very expensive). They will indicate the age of the reader, their lifestyle and the type of activities they enjoy reading about. Also most magazines won't run copy that might upset their advertisers, and that will help you decide where to send your submissions – if you are a passionate organic gardener, then don't submit to a magazine that's full of adverts for gardening chemicals.

ONE-OFF FEATURES

These are where most freelance opportunities arise, so study them carefully. Make a list of the titles, with a brief description of each one, its content and illustration. Try to work out how many were written by freelancers and how many by staffers – you may find that there is virtually no freelance work in that particular magazine, in which case it's best to start again with a different magazine.

Types of feature

There are four broad types of feature:

1 **background:** *these take a news story and explore the issues and personalities behind it in greater depth*
2 **products:** *these include product reviews, round-ups, comparisons and tests; they also include reviews of the arts and restaurants*
3 **people:** *this large category includes interviews and profiles and stories about people's lives and achievements*

4 opinion: *this includes leaders* and editorials, think pieces*, regular columns, diary columns and one-off opinion-based pieces.*

How to analyse a feature

If your analysis of the whole magazine shows that there might be an opening for the type of material you can write then it is time to analyse one feature in detail. Choose a feature that you feel you could have written and look at:

▶ *content*
▶ *vocabulary*
▶ *sentences*
▶ *paragraphs*
▶ *page furniture*
▶ *illustrations*
▶ *word count.*

CONTENT

Is the feature serious, light-hearted, informative, provocative, contentious, humorous, topical, historical?

VOCABULARY

What kind of words are used in the piece: short, long, technical, slangy? Although there are conventions for journalistic writing (see Chapter 13) there is still a huge range of possibilities. Many publications avoid long words, simply because they don't work well in columns (see below).

***leader:** an article in a prominent position at the front of a magazine, often written by the editor

***think piece:** an expression of the writer's opinion, not necessarily reflecting magazine policy

SENTENCES

Sentences are also likely to be short, if only because long sentences make for long paragraphs and long paragraphs are not desirable, but this will vary from magazine to magazine. Choose a few sentences at random and count the words. In a well-written piece there should be a variety of sentence length, because this creates a rhythm and is more interesting for the reader.

Tony Staveacre

Tony is a freelance writer and producer, working in TV, radio and theatre. He is the author of several books on popular culture, and also occasional arts journalism articles.

The trick is to find a route through the commissioning maze!

I have the sense that unsolicited articles sent by post or email rarely get read by features editors, let alone responded to. Three years ago I wrote a piece to promote a theatre show I was producing and sent it to my local paper. It happened to strike a chord with that editor, who subsequently said he'd take other stuff from me. This was the *Western Daily Press* and I've written articles for them every month for the last three years. So, find an editor and hang on to his coat-tails!

I have also had some success by responding to *The Guardian*'s feature pages, where they invite readers to contribute ('Experience' in the weekend magazine, and 'Snapshot' on the family pages). They pay a fee also.

I occasionally contribute to our local free papers – *Mendip Life*, *Mendip Times* and the *Chew Valley Gazette*. They don't pay fees, but I've managed to negotiate a free ad for my dance band, as a 'quid pro quo' for articles.

PARAGRAPHS

Newspaper and magazine paragraphs have to be short. This is because the pages are usually arranged in columns, and long paragraphs in narrow columns produce an unreadable solid body of text. Count the words in several paragraphs to find the average. The opening paragraph will probably be the shortest because it needs to grab the reader's attention. Check how many sentences there are in each par*. Some magazines may prefer only one sentence, another may like two – others may prefer three or four.

Example
The previous paragraph is 82 words long and sits quite nicely across the page. If the page were divided into two columns the paragraph would look like this:

Newspaper and magazine paragraphs have to be short. This is because the pages are arranged in columns, and long paragraphs in narrow columns produce an unreadable solid body of text. Count the words in several paragraphs to find the average. The opening paragraph will probably be the shortest because it needs to grab the reader's attention. Check how many sentences there are in each par. Some magazines may prefer only one sentence, another may like two – others may prefer three or four.

You can see at once that this paragraph is far too long.

*par: word for paragraph, used by editors in a hurry

PAGE FURNITURE

Look at how the material is laid out on the page. Is the page busy, full of different typefaces and information in small chunks, or is it rather more soberly laid out?

ILLUSTRATIONS

Examine the photographs and graphics. How important are they? Some editors are far more interested in the illustrations than the text, whereas others see illustration as no more than window dressing.

WORD COUNT

Finally, count all the words in the main body of the feature. This is a tiresome task, but worth doing once or twice to get a feel for length. A popular magazine will have an average feature length of 800 words or less, while a more heavyweight magazine will have an average of 1,500 words and occasional features running to 3,000.

Exercises
- ▶ *Choose a magazine and analyse it.*
- ▶ *Choose a feature and analyse it.*

10 THINGS TO REMEMBER

1   *Always establish that there is a market for the topic you wish to write about.*

2   *Find subscriber-only magazines on the internet.*

3   *Check out the specialist press relevant to your topic.*

4   *Always use the writers' guidelines where available.*

5   *Get a feel for the house style of your chosen magazine.*

6   *Analyse the magazine over several issues.*

7   *Try to work out which articles were written by freelancers.*

8   *Don't forget to analyse the adverts.*

9   *Most freelance opportunities are in one-off features.*

10 *Analyse several features for content, vocabulary, sentences, paragraphs and word count.*

5

Ideas

In this chapter you will learn:
- *where to find ideas for articles*
- *how to generate ideas for articles*
- *how to assess and tailor an idea.*

> *When considering material for publication I would be looking for a submission that puts a new slant or spin on good, old-fashioned advice.*
>
> Suzanne Ruthven, Editor, *The New Writer*

Ideas are the life blood of all magazines. Whereas news is driven by things that happen, and then get reported, features are created when someone has an idea and is able to develop it and write it up.

Very often it is your idea that an editor is buying rather than your writing – after all, there are competent writers on the staff and any number of other freelancers who can write as well as you. The ability to generate a constant flow of saleable ideas is therefore essential for anyone wanting to do more than write the occasional article.

Write what you know

The advice given to all beginning writers is to 'write about what you know' – and this is a good place to start with feature writing.

Not only will you feel more comfortable around the subjects you are familiar with, you will also have a lot less research to do and be able to get on with submitting work much more quickly.

For example, if your hobby is caravanning you could start by considering the small number of specialist magazines for caravanners and then consider whether any general interest magazines might be persuaded to take a feature on caravan holidays. Then there are the crossover possibilities for other specialist magazines – a piece about using a caravan to stay in remote areas for bird watching, another about a painting holiday, another about the advantages of a specially-adapted caravan for someone with disabilities.

Everyone has expertise of some sort. Look at all the areas of your life, including:

▶ **work:** *even if you are not at the top of your particular tree, you will still know something about your job that might make an article*
▶ **hobbies:** *again you don't have to be an expert on a subject to be able to write about it*
▶ **personal life:** *have you experienced something unusual or interesting?*
▶ **family:** *is there anything different about your experience of family life?*

You can see at once that writing about what you know is likely to produce two different types of feature:

▶ *expertise*
▶ *personal experience.*

EXPERTISE

These can be based on something you yourself have done or be the product of research. If you've built your own kitchen extension from scratch, you can write about your experience of doing it, and with a little research you can write a more general article about extension building. You could also extend your research and write about other types of self-building.

> **Insight**
> Keep up to date with any of the areas in which you have expertise so that you are not only coming up with new ideas but remain at the forefront of current knowledge.

PERSONAL EXPERIENCE

These are about your life experiences and don't need an element of expertise. Many magazines are looking for material about such things as massive weight loss, recovery from a life-threatening illness, or dealing with violence. On a less dramatic level, if you've fostered many children, raised a million for charity or married into a different culture you have a story to tell.

Some people feel that being paid to tell your life story is a form of exploitation. Only you can decide how you feel about this. If it makes you feel uncomfortable, then don't do it.

Generating ideas

Very few of us lead lives that are so eventful as to provide a continuous stream of article ideas; sooner or later a magazine writer will have to start generating ideas from a cold start. This is not as daunting as it sounds since we are surrounded with a constant flow of information which is full of potential ideas.

> **Insight**
> Because ideas can be triggered any time, any place – a snatch of overheard conversation or the back of someone's paper on the underground – it is important to keep a notebook handy and jot them down. For if one thing is certain, it's if you don't write them down you will forget them.

SOURCES

There are many places to look for ideas. These include:

▶ **newspapers:** *news items can be followed up in depth or spark ideas for related features. National stories may have a local angle.*

▶ **magazines:** *features in one magazine might trigger an idea which could be used in another magazine, so read as many different magazines as you can. Ask friends and family to save them for you and make the most of any time you have to spend in waiting rooms by checking out all publications – even the in-house and technical ones because ideas can come from anywhere.*

▶ **back issues:** *old issues of magazines might well have features that could be reworked in an up-to-date way. Buy them at car boot sales, but don't use them for magazine research as styles change all the time.*

▶ **adverts:** *browsing the small ads can throw up all sorts of unusual ideas.*

▶ **press releases:** *ask to be put on the mailing lists of organizations that are of interest.*

▶ **the internet:** *news groups, bulletin boards and chat rooms are all potential sources of ideas. Check the National Archives website for the latest releases of information now available to the public, which may trigger a story.*

▶ **anniversaries:** *try to pick the more unusual ones. Always look ahead – a year is not too far.*

▶ **events:** *big events stimulate interest in related subjects. For instance, a big sporting event such as the Olympics would stimulate interest in the life and culture of the host country, or a royal wedding might create interest in wedding fashions.*

▶ **contacts:** *once you have built up a contacts list, keep in touch.*

▶ **trends:** *try to get a feel for what readers are currently interested in, and try to spot new interests on the horizon.*

Insight

Check out anniversaries well in advance. There are websites that give chronologies, or try Googling the date from 10, 50, 100 or even 200 years ago.

If researching different publications doesn't produce anything inspiring, there are various mental techniques that can help you find an idea.

Pick a topic
Choose a new topic that you are interested in and research it with a view to developing several article ideas. Try to choose a topic that is broad enough to have many applications. For example, acquiring detailed knowledge of different types of car exhaust is not going to take you much further than the motoring magazines, whereas researching unusual uses for old cars might have much broader applications.

A really broad topic such as superstitions could take you into almost any magazine – there are the superstitions relating to almost all trades, those for special occasions such as weddings or Christmas, superstitions in different cultures and so on. Eventually, if you became known as the journalist with superstitions at their fingertips you might well find editors asking you for contributions.

Free thinking
Choose a topic, take a large sheet of paper, write the name of the topic in the middle and draw a circle around it. See how many associated words you can come up with, put each one in its own circle with a line connecting it to the central word. Then take each of those words and repeat the procedure, and do it again if your piece of paper is big enough. You will end up with a lot of possible ideas and connections, some of which will give you suitable angles on the central idea, and some of which will be new ideas for separate articles.

Insight
Don't try to free think on the computer, you will get a much better result with pen and paper.

Free association
This is allowing the brain to wander at will. You need to be physically relaxed, in the bath or lying down, and you need to

be able to let go of all your everyday worries and thoughts. It might help to listen to a relaxation or self-hypnosis CD. Just let your mind drift and see where it takes you. Don't forget to have pen and paper nearby to write down the results.

Internet browsing
Using a search engine, tap in a subject and then follow all the websites which come up. For each website, explore related websites and links; when you reach a page that looks interesting, download it for future reference.

Insight
Curiosity is one of the main drivers in successful journalism. The writer has to be constantly curious to seek out the most interesting stories. In turn, these excite curiosity in the reader, making them want to read more.

Assessing an idea

Not all ideas are suitable for development into features. Some are so big they need a book, while some don't have enough potential for depth. Some are so contentious they will never find a home, while others require access to people or information that a freelancer is unlikely to get. And inevitably there are fashions in magazine content – try leafing through a back copy of any magazine and you will find topics that are no longer of interest. An idea needs to be around a subject that is currently interesting but not overexposed.

Anyone who is trying to earn a living with their writing will also have to consider how much time to devote to researching the article if it hasn't been commissioned – and few writers are commissioned at the start of their careers although it is something everyone should aim for.

We've already seen that some ideas (car exhausts) are too specialized to have much of a market, although if it happened to be something you know about anyway, it might be worth trying one article in a specialist magazine precisely because you wouldn't have to spend a lot of time on research.

Tailoring an idea

A simple idea may get you started on an article, but to get an editor to take it you will also need to make it unique and compelling. This is done by using:

- ▶ *angles*
- ▶ *slanting*
- ▶ *hooks*
- ▶ *pegs*
- ▶ *human interest.*

ANGLES

There are various ways of finding a new angle for a story:

- ▶ **focus in:** *if your idea is to write a piece about stately homes then focus in on the subject by concentrating on those which have been used as films sets or for television series. An alternative is to cover all the stately homes in a certain area.*
- ▶ **broaden the scope:** *using the same idea, expand it to include the most popular stately homes in several European countries.*
- ▶ **use a well-known format:** *such as 'Top Ten Stately Homes' or the 'Rough Guide to Stately Homes'.*
- ▶ **link it to another subject:** *taking famous paintings as a starting point, write about the houses featured in them.*

SLANTING

Slanting an article is similar to finding an angle but it specifically relates to making the same idea appealing to more than one type of magazine. This is particularly useful if you have assembled a mass of information about an idea because if one magazine turns it down you can use a different slant and send it somewhere else.

For example, using stately homes as the starting point concentrate on:

▸ *their gardens for gardening magazines*
▸ *their kitchens for household and cookery magazines*
▸ *their history for educational magazines.*

HOOKS

These are the means of engaging the reader's (and the editor's) interest in an article. The hook is used in the opening paragraph. Using the above example, which might be a bit dry for many readers, the hook could be the notorious inhabitants of the stately homes, scandalous events in the past or contemporary ones such as rock concerts or weddings.

PEGS

These are sometimes also called hooks and are similar to them. However, pegs link the idea to something specific such as a time of year, or a person or an activity. In the above example a peg could be how Christmas is celebrated in various stately homes.

HUMAN INTEREST

There will always be more than one potential angle for an idea and you will have to choose the one most likely to result in a sale. This will depend on its suitability for a particular publication and your access to the research facilities required. For all but the most technical publications, the key here is human interest. If you can find the human interest element in your idea then you greatly increase your chances of making a sale.

Work in progress

Recent changes in the law on smoking have led to a lot of media interest in the topic so an article about smoking is likely to find a market in a wide range of magazines.

Possible angles include focusing on smokers huddled in the rain outside their office, broadening the subject to look at smoking laws in other countries, using the format of 'Ten Top Ways to Quit' or linking to the subject of civil liberties.

The obvious hook for any smoking article will be human interest, whether it is people who are trying to quit or those whose jobs are threatened by the change in the law. An interesting peg could be the way smoking featured in old black and white movies, or smoking traditions.

Exercises
- *List your areas of expertise.*
- *List your interesting personal experiences.*
- *Make a list of possible new topics to research.*
- *Brainstorm around one of the topics from your expertise, experience or from something new to you.*
- *Do free association around a different topic.*
- *Browse the internet on another topic.*
- *Assess the three topics you have explored.*

10 THINGS TO REMEMBER

1 *All magazines need a constant flow of ideas for articles.*

2 *Start with what you know.*

3 *Consider all your areas of expertise.*

4 *Don't forget your personal experiences.*

5 *Learn to generate ideas from a cold start.*

6 *Explore all possible sources of ideas.*

7 *Use mental techniques to spark new ideas.*

8 *Assess all ideas for their suitability.*

9 *Find a way to make your idea unique and compelling.*

10 *The most important quality an idea needs is human interest.*

6

Proposals and submissions

In this chapter you will learn:
- *how to create a proposal*
- *how to submit an article*
- *how to tailor your CV.*

> *It's been said many times, but it still needs saying – the four words that will send your piece straight into the bin are: 'Dear Sir or Madam'. If you can't even be bothered to find out the name of the editor, you really shouldn't be in this business at all.*
>
> Gill Hudson, former Editor, *Radio Times*

Writers can approach editors with either an idea for an article (a proposal) or a finished article (a submission on spec*). Editors on the whole prefer proposals because they are too busy to read articles submitted on spec – but check their guidelines. Until you have a track record they may ask you to write the article without being commissioned, but this does not mean that they are committed to taking your article, only that they will look at it and then make a decision. Of course, if you write the article and it is rejected you can then submit it elsewhere.

On small publications the approach is made direct to the editor; in larger organizations there will be a commissioning editor who is responsible for dealing with submissions and proposals, and who will then pass their choices to the editor or editorial team for approval.

***on spec:** sending an already written article without being commissioned

If you are a hobby writer you can send proposals out one at a time, as the feeling takes you, but if you are attempting to make a living by writing, you will need to maintain a constant flow of proposals and submissions to many different publications. Allocate time every day to tracking their progress and generating new ones. It's been said that a freelance journalist needs to have a hundred ideas with editors at any one time, and while this is an exaggeration you certainly need to maintain the momentum.

Note that this is not the same as making multiple submissions of an article. Editors don't like this and it is not good practice. The only time it is acceptable is if you have an article that is time-sensitive and on a short time scale (but remember that in magazine terms this can mean three months or more). In that case you can make multiple submissions but mention in your covering letter that you are doing so. However, there is nothing to stop you sending out multiple copies of a proposal.

Insight

If you are planning to write humorous articles – or any article where the style is the most important aspect – then it is worth sending one as a sample, but you may be asked to write on a completely different topic.

Sending a proposal

Carry out some initial research into your idea, enough to be sure that you can produce an article from it. Once you have researched the market, it is time to make contact with the magazine of your choice.

PHONE, LETTER OR EMAIL?

The contents page of the magazine will usually give an email address, but this is almost always intended for readers to make contact, not freelance writers. Magazine entries in the *Writers' and Artists' Yearbook* very rarely give email addresses in the contact details – indicating that most editors prefer not to be emailed.

If you do send an email, set your software to request a 'Read Receipt' so you will know that the email has arrived – although this only works if the recipient returns the receipt.

The best way to make an initial approach is by phone. Complete your preparation work before you make the call – following all the steps for preparing a query letter given below. If you are put straight through to someone, you will be prepared and able to talk them through your idea. Start by asking how the magazine prefers writers to pitch an idea.

However, it is most likely that you will be told to write in with your proposal. Editors like to look at written proposals because they can do it in their own time, and it shows them straight away whether you can write.

Insight

Always ask for the name of the person you should send your proposal to, and double-check the spelling of the name. Also ask for their correct job title and its spelling if necessary.

Written proposals

A written proposal must be immaculate – remember it is your calling card. It should consist of:

- *a query letter*
- *a CV*
- *cuttings.*

THE QUERY LETTER

It is best to follow a simple format for a query letter. Keep it to one page. Address the editor by name. Start with a simple sentence saying that you are a writer with an idea, followed by a paragraph summarizing your article and mentioning the length. If you have done your magazine research or obtained the magazine's guidelines, you will know how long the article should be. Also mention any special research or contacts and say if you are providing illustrations.

The next paragraph should say why the magazine's readers would be interested in the article, and show that you know the magazine hasn't covered this topic. The final paragraph should briefly say something about your qualifications to write the article and what rights you are offering (see Chapter 8 for more information on rights).

One word of warning about query letters, keep them straightforward and serious – if you are a humorous writer, never attempt to write a comedy query letter. It looks amateurish.

Example
A query letter for an article about giving up smoking:

Dear Ann Gawthorpe

Would you be interested in an article about the various techniques for giving up smoking?

The article will explain how different techniques are suitable for different people, with case histories and information about each technique. The main text will be 1,500 words.

As I know from the Letters pages of recent issues, many of your readers are smokers so I believe this article would be of great interest to them. I notice that while you have covered many aspects of modern life you have not featured smoking.

I am a stress counsellor and I write occasionally for newsletters and company magazines (see enclosed cuttings).

I am offering First British Serial Rights.

(Contd)

TAILORING A CV

A new writer might feel they have nothing to put on a CV, but it is worthwhile taking some time to compile one and eventually you will have writing credits to add to it.

There are some 'dos and don'ts' for writing a good CV:

- ▶ *Type it, don't handwrite it.*
- ▶ *Keep it to one page.*
- ▶ *Use white or cream paper with a simple font such as Ariel or Times New Roman.*
- ▶ *Start with your name, address, phone number, email address and mobile number.*
- ▶ *Give your age, race, marital status and number of children only if they are relevant to the type of article you intend writing. For example, if you want to write about teenage angst, the fact that you have two teenage children will give authority to your writing and make it more saleable. Otherwise leave this information out.*
- ▶ *List your relevant educational achievements and exams passed. If you intend writing about furniture restoration then it is relevant to mention your A-level in woodwork.*
- ▶ *List all relevant hobbies, interests and activities with any clubs and societies you belong to and any positions you hold – but again only mention those which relate to the type of article you intend to write.*
- ▶ *List any relevant jobs or professional appointments.*
- ▶ *List your writing activities so far (remembering to add to this with each new achievement).*

- ▶ *Don't waffle; keep it short, succinct and easily readable.*
- ▶ *Don't use fancy gimmicks or fancy layouts or photographs.*
- ▶ *Don't rely on a computer spellchecker; read it through carefully to check for errors.*

CUTTINGS PORTFOLIO

If you have followed our advice in Chapter 2 to build up your skills, you should now have a collection of cuttings. Once you start to have successes as a paid writer, always keep everything that you have published, even the small items. Your complete collection will serve as a reference so that you don't repeat yourself – and also an ego boost on the dark days when it seems like you are getting nothing but rejections.

When you remove a cutting from a publication always take the whole page, so that you include the header or footer where the name of the publication and the date are shown. When you are submitting a proposal make photocopies of one or two cuttings and include them with the letter. Never send the originals as they probably won't be returned to you.

Insight
If you are invited to visit the magazine's offices to discuss your proposal, take your portfolio of the most important and relevant cuttings with you.

Submitting on spec

Submitting on spec means that you have done all the work for an article without knowing whether you will be paid for it. Never submit a draft or half-finished article in the hope that the editor will tell you how to finish it or commission you to finish it. Only send your best work, because your reputation rests on the work you send, not on the work that's still in your head.

On the whole, editors are not keen on being sent complete articles that they haven't asked for, simply because they are usually too busy to read them. However, if you are a beginner or the article is already written and you have faith in it, then send it off. Include a covering letter that is so well written that the editor can't resist reading the article too.

If you want the article returned to you, you should enclose return postage. Editors have different opinions as to whether this is a good idea – some see it as professional, others say it shows a lack of confidence. However, if your article has been generated on a computer it is unlikely you will need it returned.

Exercises
- ▶ *Choose a promising topic from the previous chapter's exercises. Look for a topic that requires research and interviews so that you can use it in later exercises. Ideally you should pick one where you can interview an existing contact who will be willing to do you a favour at this early stage in your career.*
- ▶ *Write a proposal letter for it.*
- ▶ *Post the letter if you wish.*

10 THINGS TO REMEMBER

1 *Editors usually prefer proposals but always check the Writers' Guidelines.*

2 *Keep track of your proposals; record who you sent them to and what the response was.*

3 *Making multiple submissions of an article is not good practice.*

4 *Editors like to see a written proposal as it will show them whether you can write.*

5 *Your proposal must be immaculate.*

6 *Keep your query letter simple and avoid humorous remarks.*

7 *Include a CV that is tailored to the particular proposal.*

8 *Include one or two photocopies of cuttings from your portfolio of work.*

9 *Never submit a draft or half-finished article.*

10 *Make sure you correctly spell the name of the person you are sending them to.*

7

Response to submissions and proposals

In this chapter you will learn:
- *about the four possible outcomes*
- *how to deal with rejection*
- *about the risk of an idea being stolen.*

> *If I had to offer a single nugget of advice it would be get to know your editor's quirks and foibles. Get it right and your material will always be read with a sympathetic eye.*
>
> Suzanne Ruthven, Editor, *The New Writer*

Outcomes

There are four possible outcomes to a submission or proposal:

- *nothing happens*
- *rejection*
- *conditional acceptance*
- *acceptance.*

NOTHING HAPPENS

If an editor is not interested in your proposal, the most likely outcome is that they will ignore it. This is frustrating for the writer who wants to know one way or the other. Even if they've been rejected, most people want to know why. However, writers have to accept that editors are busy and rarely have time to respond to unwanted ideas. They are also human and may not like sending rejections.

However, there are other reasons why the writer might not hear anything, for example:

▶ *the proposal has gone astray and not reached the editor*
▶ *the editor does not like this particular proposal but does not have time to respond and ask for something else*
▶ *you have submitted the wrong type of proposal for the magazine*
▶ *if you have submitted an article rather than a proposal, your writing isn't good enough.*

Insight

Do not spend too long agonizing over what might or might not have been going through an editor's mind – you are wasting valuable writing time. Move on and come up with more ideas.

After two or three weeks, if you have had no response, write, email or phone and politely check that the article or proposal was received. It is also worthwhile saying that if it is not what the editor was looking for, you have other ideas. If the editor expresses an interest in your other ideas then submit fresh proposals. If they still do not respond then you must assume that either you are submitting to the wrong magazine or that your writing is not up to scratch.

If it is the wrong magazine, look for a more suitable one. If you think it is your writing, don't ask the editor what is wrong with it – it is not up to them to improve your style – go back to the drawing board and rewrite it.

It is best not to send this improved piece to the same editor (unless they have specifically asked you to do so). Submit it elsewhere.

REJECTION

Rejection is part and parcel of being a freelance writer and has
to be accepted. If you find rejection hard to take, then perhaps
freelance writing is not for you. Properly used, rejection can have
a beneficial effect. It can spur you to improve your writing or find
other outlets for your articles.

Magazine rejections are usually short and to the point, for
example: 'Thank you for your suggestion but it is not for us at the
moment.'

It is very rare indeed for an editor to give any clue as to why a
proposal is rejected and you should never phone or write asking
for an explanation. In other words, you will never know if your
proposal was ludicrously bad, wonderfully good but too similar
to another one already in development, too long, too short, or
any one of a number of other possibilities. If you do receive any
feedback, count yourself lucky and try to take it on board.

It has to be said that luck does play a part in whether a piece is
accepted or rejected. If you send in an idea on the changing shape
of wash basins over the past 100 years just when the editor was
thinking of including a feature on the history of bathrooms there is
a chance yours may be accepted.

In a sense we all make our own luck. The harder you work, and the more proposals you send out, the more chance you have of getting lucky.

Example

Lesley sent a proposal to a national magazine for an article about gardening. She received an immediate response by email:

> *Hi*
>
> *Just to confirm that your information has been gratefully received and has now been forwarded to our Gardening Editor for consideration – if she is interested in following this up, she will contact you directly and let you know.*
>
> *Thanks for taking the trouble to contact us and thinking of our publication.*
>
> *With kind regards*
>
> *Editorial*

After three weeks another email arrived:

> *Thank you for sending me this idea which I was interested to see. Unfortunately, as you will have noticed we don't have that much room in the magazine for gardening and what we have is filled already for the foreseeable future.*
>
> *Thank you for thinking of us.*
>
> *Yours*
>
> *Editor at Large*

CONDITIONAL ACCEPTANCE

The editor may like the look of your proposal but if you have no track record they'll feel unsure about your ability to deliver the goods. They'll give you a response along the lines of 'write it up and we'll have a look at it.' The good news is that you're in with a chance; the bad news is that you won't get paid unless the final piece is accepted.

This is a great opportunity for a beginner. If the editor doesn't take the finished piece they will probably feel they ought to tell you why, so at the very least you'll be able to learn something from the experience.

For an established writer conditional acceptance is far less appealing and if there is other work on the horizon it can be politely declined.

Because the piece has not been officially commissioned, you will not be able to tell potential interviewees or anyone else with useful information that you are writing a piece for that magazine. However, you can say that you are writing a piece that an editor has expressed an interest in and that you hope will be accepted.

ACCEPTANCE

If your proposal is accepted, you will probably get a phone call or an email. If it's a phone call it's important to make notes as you talk – your main task is to establish the brief*, but you should also not be afraid to talk about your fee and expenses, and to ask to have this in writing (see Chapter 8 for more on this). Very few magazines issue contracts, although some of the bigger ones do.

Insight

After the excitement of being accepted, remember this is when the real work starts – you still have to deliver an article that is up to standard, and within the deadline.

*brief: an editor's requirements for an article

Stolen ideas

Sometimes you will have your proposal rejected only to see a similar feature in the magazine some time later. Was your idea stolen? Probably not, although the truth is that you will never know for sure. It is more likely that someone had a similar idea to you at about the same time. In any case, there is no copyright on ideas. You can achieve a measure of protection when you submit your proposal by keeping back the names of contacts and any special access to research that you have.

If, however, a magazine uses your actual words, taken from an article you submitted on spec, then you do have recourse in law. In practice very few writers pursue this; in any case it is a rare occurrence.

Occasionally an editor will ask a more experienced writer to develop your idea and – if they are honourable – they will tell you and even pay you for the idea. This means that your idea was a good one, so keep your temper and ask if you might be given a chance to write it up next time.

Exercise
▶ *Rewrite your proposal letter for another magazine.*

10 THINGS TO REMEMBER

1 *Possible outcomes to a submission or proposal are: nothing happens, rejection, conditional acceptance and acceptance.*

2 *If nothing happens – even after sending a reminder – then move on.*

3 *Rejection happens to everyone, so learn to deal with it, and learn from it.*

4 *If you sent a submission or proposal to the wrong magazine, find the right one.*

5 *Conditional acceptance isn't ideal but it is still a chance of publication.*

6 *Luck may play a part in whether a proposal is accepted or rejected.*

7 *Other writers may well have had the same idea as you.*

8 *Don't be afraid to ask for expenses.*

9 *There is no copyright on ideas.*

10 *If a magazine uses your actual words, then you do have recourse in law.*

8

Considering commissions

In this chapter you will learn:
- *about briefs*
- *about deadlines*
- *about rights.*

> *If you're thinking of writing for publication – and that's why most people write articles – you need to give the editor what he/she wants – so this means researching the market.*
>
> Jan Barwick, Editor, *Devon Life*

The brief

The brief is the list of requirements the editor wants in your article and can be written or verbal. However, editors vary as to how much time and effort they are prepared to put into a brief and freelancers may not be given much more than the number of words required. If possible, the brief should specify the following about the article:

- ▶ *the deadline for delivery of the manuscript*
- ▶ *the means of delivery (such as hard copy, email, disk, CD-ROM)*
- ▶ *the length of the article*
- ▶ *the angle or approach required*

- *the tone (e.g. light-hearted, informative, provocative)*
- *the scope (e.g. anything that must be included or omitted)*
- *any extras such as tables, photographs, charts and illustrations.*

Insight

Editors will often commission more articles than they need for a given issue. You must work to the deadline, but you can't be sure of publication. If it doesn't get used, you can send it to another suitable magazine.

Get as much information as you can about how the editor sees the article. After the call, write up your notes and send them to the editor so that any misunderstandings can be cleared up. Mention any changes that were made to your original proposal so the editor knows you have taken them on board. If you were accepted by email, then discuss the brief by email or phone the editor to talk it through.

Insight

Once you have started work, you may find that your research pulls you in a different direction from the original brief. Always check this with the editor.

Factors to consider

When you are negotiating a commission, there are various practical aspects to bear in mind. These include:

- *deadlines*
- *time management*
- *word counts*
- *illustrations*
- *rights*
- *payment*
- *kill fee*
- *expenses.*

DEADLINES

Don't imagine that article writing can be fitted in to odd free moments, because you will be expected to work to a deadline. All magazines work to a complicated series of deadlines and your article is only one small part of that. If you send in something on spec, and it is accepted, then of course your work is already done and the editor will simply file the article away ready to be slotted in to the relevant edition. But if you send in a proposal and are commissioned then you will be given a deadline for delivery of the article and you will have to meet it.

It helps to have an understanding of the complexity of magazine production. All the written material has to be assembled and coordinated with the necessary illustrations. The basic steps are:

▶ *edit*
▶ *page make-up*
▶ *typeset*
▶ *go to press*
▶ *distribute.*

Because of this complexity, deadlines for features are always some way ahead of the appearance of the magazine:

▶ **features for newspapers:** *two to four weeks*
▶ **weekly magazines:** *six to twelve weeks*
▶ **monthly magazines:** *three to six months*
▶ **quarterly magazines:** *six to twelve months.*

Special editions work even further ahead than that, with Christmas editions having the longest lead time* of all.

If you agree to a deadline, whether it is next week or next year, you must stick to it. Editors simply won't use you again if you are unreliable, in fact they probably won't even use the article you sent in late, and you won't be paid for it.

*lead time: the time allowed to produce a magazine

TIME MANAGEMENT

If you plan to write only the occasional article then you won't need to worry too much about organizing your time, but if you want to produce a steady flow of work then you will need to be disciplined about it. This is particularly the case if you have a lot of other commitments.

It is important to be realistic about your ability to deliver. Only you know how much time and energy you have. If an editor phones to say they love your idea and can you deliver by the end of next week, don't agree in a moment of excitement at being commissioned. Think for a moment. How much research still needs to be done? How many sources do you need to contact? How quickly do you write? How much time do you have in the coming week?

The simplest way to manage your time is to construct a series of deadlines for yourself, for example:

- ▶ **four weeks before deadline:** *finish research*
- ▶ **three weeks before deadline:** *write first draft*
- ▶ **two weeks before deadline:** *write second draft*
- ▶ **ten days before deadline:** *double-check facts*
- ▶ **nine days before deadline:** *final polish*
- ▶ **one week before deadline:** *deliver.*

You may prefer, or be obliged, to work to a tighter deadline than this, but it shows that the main flexibility is in the length of time you spend on the research. If your delivery deadline is some months away then you have a lot of time for research, but if it is only five weeks away then you have very little. Remember that time is money and the fee for the article probably won't compensate you for the hours spent on research. (Research is only truly cost effective if it can be used for more than one article.)

WORD COUNTS

If your brief specifies a particular number of words then you must stick to that. The editor will know to within a word or two how much space they can give an article on a page and won't thank you if you ignore the requested number of words. If there is no number specified, then ask.

ILLUSTRATIONS

If you have agreed to provide illustrations or photographs then you will need a separate timetable to be sure they meet the deadline too. See Chapter 18 for more on illustration.

RIGHTS

You own the copyright in everything that you write, and when you sell it to a magazine you are actually selling them the right to use your words. The basic right that you usually sell is called First British Serial Rights (FBSR) or First American Serial Rights (FASR).

Strictly speaking it is possible to sell Second British Serial Rights, where a magazine will reprint an article that has already appeared elsewhere. In practice this very rarely happens in Britain. In America this is more common because many regional publications are happy to take second rights on an article.

It is quite common to sell an article abroad which has already appeared in another country. You must tell the publication that the article has already been published, and where, but then you can sell them the First Serial Rights.

There is often pressure from publishers for you to sell them All Rights, which effectively means they own the article for all time. They should of course pay you more for this. It means they can put your article on their website (which is a money-earning tool for them) or in any other medium that is developed in the future. Only you can say whether you are prepared to part with these rights.

Electronic rights
These are the right to publish articles in a digital form on the internet, CD-ROMs, disks and so on, and, as the writer, you own these rights until you sell them to someone else. If you sign

a contract selling your FBSR or FASR check to see if any electronic rights have been included and whether you are happy with this.

When it comes to downloading articles onto e-zine websites it is worth checking to see what other rights you are giving away because you may want to send the article to a magazine as well. If you can't find any information about this on the site then contact the site owner and ask.

Because ownership of electronic rights is a comparatively new area, and has been the subject of several court cases, the legalities of ownership are outside the remit of this book.

Subsidiary rights

In Britain, the Authors' Licensing and Collecting Society (ALCS) collects various subsidiary rights for writers. The main one of interest to journalists is photocopying, in which various institutions, such as universities, pay a blanket fee for the right to photocopy whatever they need.

This money is shared out every year between all the writers who are registered with ALCS and who qualify for payment. There is a small fee for registering (currently £10), although it is free to members of some writers' organizations.

You will have to send ALCS a list of all the articles you have had published, along with their word count, the name of the publication and the publication's ISSN* number.

Insight

Don't overlook ALCS payments – sometimes they can double what you've earned from an article, and with small magazines that don't pay at all, the ALCS payment will be your only income.

*ISSN: International Standard Serial Number. It can usually be found on the contents page along with the volume number and the issue number.

PAYMENT

Don't be embarrassed about discussing payment with an editor. Ask what their normal rates are or how much they are prepared to pay for the article, and when you will be paid. There are two basic types of payment: POA (payment on acceptance) and POP (payment on publication). Payment on acceptance means you get paid even if, for some reason, the article isn't used. Payment on publication could mean waiting some time for your money, particularly if there is a long lead time.

KILL FEE

The kill fee is the amount you will be paid if, for any reason, the article isn't used. Always discuss it before accepting the commission. Even if there isn't one, it's better for you to know that up front. A kill fee for a POP article needs to be higher than a POA article.

EXPENSES

If you have submitted a proposal, generally speaking your expenses won't be met as it will be assumed they are covered by the payment for the article. If your expenses are going to be high because, for example, you have had to pay a large sum for copyright permission, then it is worthwhile asking whether the magazine is prepared to meet any of them. Once you are an established writer you may find editors approaching you to ask you to take on an article – in which case you should always ask for expenses.

Syndication

This means running an article or regular column in more than one publication. It is rare in the UK simply because of geography – in a small country editors will consider it likely that readers may well see both magazines carrying the same article. In the US it is far more common for successful writers to be able to syndicate their work. They can either do this themselves or through a specialist agency which will take part of the payment for the article.

Exercise
▶ *Plan a timetable for writing your article.*

10 THINGS TO REMEMBER

1 *The brief describes the article, the deadline and the means of delivery.*

2 *If the brief is verbal, confirm it in writing.*

3 *Create a timetable for work on the article to ensure you meet the deadline.*

4 *Deadlines for some magazines can be up to a year ahead of publication.*

5 *Create a separate timetable for organizing the illustrations, if needed.*

6 *Make sure you understand your Rights in the article.*

7 *Electronic rights are increasingly important.*

8 *Establish when and how much you will be paid.*

9 *Negotiate for a kill fee.*

10 *Negotiate for expenses.*

9

Researching information

In this chapter you will learn:
- *about sources*
- *about research tools*
- *about plagiarism and copyright.*

> *The internet's limitless appetite for user-generated content means there's more opportunity for a newcomer to get their work out to a wider audience than there was before.*
>
> Gill Hudson, former Editor, *Radio Times*

Very few articles can be written without any research. Even one describing your personal experience is likely to need some fact-checking.

Sources

Research is done through two types of source: primary and secondary. Primary sources are originals – whether you talk to a person who was there at the time, or examine a document, such as a bill of sale or house deeds, that was created at the time. Secondary sources are people who weren't there but who heard about the event, as well as reports (including newspapers), books written on the subject and so on.

Both can be unreliable. Witnesses don't always remember events accurately, clerks make mistakes even in legal documents, newspaper reporters make mistakes and authors can take a mistake from a source and use it in all good faith, passing it on down the line.

Always get as close to a primary source in your research as you can, and cross-check as far as possible. Information from only one primary source will always be suspect. A single mistake can become regarded as fact over time as it is passed on. This is called an error of transmission.

> **Example**
> We all know that Cinderella wore glass slippers when she went to the ball, but in the original story she wore fur slippers. The error occurred when the story was translated from the French.

Insight

If you are not sure about the quality of the information but you still want to use it, qualify it with phrases such as 'it is believed that...' or 'some people say that...'.

Techniques

Whether you are researching a topic you already have some knowledge of, or starting from scratch, the basic technique is the same – get as much background information as possible and then, if necessary, decide whom you need to interview.

By getting the background detail first you will be in a better position to ask the right questions and you will also be able to understand the answers. If circumstances force you to do the interview first, ask as many questions as you can think of, and then ask if you can come back with supplementary questions when you have had a chance to do the research.

Some sources, such as a private library or a reclusive individual, can be too difficult to access within the time available, so focus on those sources that you can access. A combination of eyewitness accounts and expert opinion or explanation will give your research balance. Using more than one source will enable you to cross-check for reliability. If apparently sound sources contradict each other then you will have to mention both to avoid bias.

Insight

In interviews you can check for reliability by asking a couple of questions that you already know the answers to. Also return to a topic and see if the interviewee tells basically the same story.

Research tools

There are many tools to help you research your ideas, including:

- *the internet*
- *libraries*
- *public record offices*
- *public records*
- *professional researchers*
- *national newspapers*
- *local newspapers*
- *magazines*
- *cuttings agencies*
- *PR agencies and press offices*
- *personal contact*
- *legwork.*

THE INTERNET

If you have access to the internet it will probably be your first port of call. Unless you know which specific website you want, use a search engine to find which websites hold the information you want. These include Google (www.google.com) and Yahoo! (www.yahoo.com). Each engine searches for information in a slightly different way so it is worth trying more than one. Then there are search engines which search other search engines, such as Ask Jeeves (www.askjeeves.co.uk) which is a United Kingdom engine and All Search Engines (www.allsearchengines.com).

One site which nearly always comes up on search engines is Wikipedia. Claimed to be the largest multinational free content encyclopaedia in the world, the information on Wikipedia is uploaded by volunteers from around the globe. But beware – information on the internet has been uploaded by all kinds of people. Some of them undoubtedly will have expert knowledge and a genuine reason for making it available to everyone. Others may think what they are saying is accurate but may have got it wrong. A few may be deliberately putting out erroneous facts.

If you use false or incorrect information in your articles, you will not only make a fool of yourself, but you may be sued. You can safeguard yourself to some extent by checking as many websites as possible for the same information. However, it is no guarantee that if the same information is shown on them all it is correct – they may all have got this knowledge from the same incorrect source.

If you are confident that you have got the correct information make sure that you keep a name and note of all the websites you have used. Sometimes you may have to pay to use copyrighted information.

If you are researching historical articles there are several websites which give access to the UK censuses from 1841 to 1901, electoral rolls, old telephone directories, armed services records, births, deaths and marriages records, ship passenger lists and so on. Some information is available for free and the rest has to be paid for. These sites are usually reliable because they are uploading their information direct from the original records.

LIBRARIES

Even the smallest library will have a non-fiction section. If it does not have the book you want, it can probably be ordered from another branch. To save time use online catalogues and order library books on the internet. Some public library authorities have subscribed to online research facilities (such as the Oxford Reference websites) and have made these available to their members for free. Once you have the password and a pin number you can even use your home computer to access them.

For more specialist subjects it will be necessary to go to a central reference library, which will have a far bigger selection. These books and documents have to be looked at in situ. Reference libraries only have limited seating areas, so it may be necessary to book a place in advance. You will probably be asked for identification and the purpose of your visit. Some books will be available on the shelves, others will have to be collected by the librarian from the archives. If you are not sure which books you will need don't be afraid to ask the librarian for help.

Be careful taking notes. Most libraries will only let you use pencils to ensure precious books and documents don't get damaged. Some documents are only available on microfiche or microfilm.

Insight

As with using information from the internet make a note of the name of the book, the author the publisher and the ISBN* in case you have to attribute information to them.

PUBLIC RECORD OFFICES

Every county has a Public Record Office housing thousands of books and old documents. These could include church registers, parish council minutes, old court records, old maps and history books of the area, as well as collections of family documents, diaries, post cards, agricultural records and so on. More and more

*ISBN: International Standard Book Number – a unique number by which any book can be identified.

are putting their catalogues online so that it is possible to see what information is held there before visiting.

As with reference libraries, there is usually limited space so it is advisable to book in advance. Checking the catalogue online in advance and noting down the reference numbers of the documents you need will also save time when you get there. If the archivists have time they might be willing to get out some documents ready for when you arrive, so give them the reference number(s) when you book your seat. As with some libraries you may only be allowed to use pencils to take notes, but there will be photocopying facilities. Always ask if you can use your camera.

If you want to use any of the documents in your article, particularly if you have taken photos to illustrate your article, you will probably need permission from the Record Office as many of the documents will be in copyright.

PUBLIC RECORDS

These include birth, death and marriage certificates, wills, council minutes, planning applications etc. Some may be available online; others will have to be applied for to the relevant authorities.

Insight

The Freedom of Information Act 2000 gives journalists the opportunity to access information held by public authorities, with certain provisos. Bodies must reply within 20 working days, or else explain why it's taking longer.

PROFESSIONAL RESEARCHERS

If the information you are looking for is only available a long way away, it might be more cost-effective to ask a professional researcher to find it for you rather than spending time and money on travelling. Public Record Office websites sometimes have links to lists of independent researchers.

NATIONAL NEWSPAPERS

The major archive for newspapers is the British Library at Colindale, North London, which holds a vast collection of newspapers and magazines. You can check their catalogue online.

Some papers such as the *Daily Telegraph* have their own online archive which allows you to look at past stories.

LOCAL NEWSPAPERS

They will hold back copies for the past year or two which can be viewed at their offices. Older copies are often microfilmed and can be viewed at the reference library. More and more local papers have an archive section on their websites where more recent back copies can be viewed.

MAGAZINES

Some will have one or two years' back copies on their websites and many make back copies available for a charge. There are also back-issue suppliers that will charge to send you copies.

CUTTINGS AGENCIES

If you have a specific story in mind, then cuttings agencies may be able to give you information from newspaper stories, but you will have to pay.

PR AGENCIES AND PRESS OFFICES

Many organizations have their own press offices and those which don't will often employ a public relations (or PR) agency to handle their publicity. There is a subtle difference between them. While both should be hoping for some free positive publicity for their organization or client, a PR agency is more likely to be proactive in trying to persuade you to say what they want. Press officers are there simply to reply to requests for information and for this reason they are mainly found in very large companies that have the resources for this, as well as government and non-governmental organizations.

Insight

To achieve balance it is a good idea to ask for information from organizations or individuals that you know have different or opposing agendas.

PERSONAL CONTACT

Start with your contact book and see if there is anyone who might be able to help you with your current research, or even pass you on to a contact of theirs. If you draw a blank with your known contacts, try cold calling*.

LEGWORK

If the subject of your article is related to one particular location then try to visit it if possible. It will add to the atmosphere of your writing if you have experienced the sight, sound and smell of the place – and you may be able to pick up nuggets of information by chatting informally to local people. If there is time, putting a small ad in the local paper asking for information or memories can yield good results (use the 'Personal' or 'Information Wanted' sections).

OTHER

The BBC has an extensive archive of information relating to broadcasting going back to 1922. Many large companies also maintain archives of company history.

---

*cold calling: phoning, or visiting a person or organization that you have not previously dealt with

Copyright

The copyright of everything that you read will belong to someone unless it is more than 70 years since the author died. To safeguard yourself from legal action try to find several different sources for the same material and then rewrite everything in your own words.

PLAGIARISM AND WRITTEN QUOTATIONS

Plagiarism means taking other people's ideas and using them without acknowledgement. If your research throws up something that is clearly common knowledge or in the public domain then you can use it, but if you find something that is clearly unique to that author then you must acknowledge both the author and your source. Always keep records of your sources.

> **Example**
> William the Conqueror's invasion in 1066 is common knowledge. An article giving detailed analysis of the food carried on the boats when they sailed across the channel is not common knowledge. If you use that information you must acknowledge your source.

APPLYING FOR PERMISSION

If you copy out someone's exact words, and plan to use them in your article then you must observe the rules known as 'fair dealing'. This means that it is usually acceptable to use short quotes taken from another writer's work without asking permission, even though strictly speaking the words are in copyright, provided you attribute the quote to the original author or source. For longer quotes you must get the written permission of the author and this can take a while. If the author is dead you still need to get permission from their estate for 70 years after their death.

Start by writing to the publisher of the book, magazine or newspaper stating what you want to quote and where it will be quoted.

Example

A sample permissions letter.

> *Permissions Department*
> *(Address)*
> *Dear Sir/Madam,*
>
> *I would like to request permission to quote the attached extract, which appeared in your publication: [give the title, author/editor, date of publication, page number].*
>
> *I would like to use this material in my forthcoming article, the details of which are as follows:*
>
> *Author:*
> *Title of article:*
> *Magazine:*
> *Estimated publication date:*
> *Rights: [UK and Commonwealth/World/etc.]*
>
> *[For short extracts] As the extract is so short I hope there will be no charge for its use. I would appreciate your letting me know if I need to apply to any other copyright holders for any or all of the rights requested. I will, of course, credit the extract and should you require a specific form of wording, would be happy to include it.*
>
> *I look forward to hearing from you at your earliest opportunity.*
>
> *Yours faithfully, etc.*

Insight

If you need to apply for permission to quote, do it early on. Many copyright owners are very slow to respond to these requests. You also need to know whether you will have to pay for this as it could affect whether you will want to use it.

Work in progress

We did the following research into smoking:

- *checked the internet for background information and statistics*
- *applied to pharmaceutical companies for press packs*
- *contacted local therapists*
- *contacted individuals for their case studies.*

Putting the words 'smoking', 'cigarettes' and 'smoking statistics' into a search engine threw up dozens of useful sites including ASH, Cancer Research UK, National Statistics online and several sites which listed the harmful ingredients in cigarettes.

We did the same with pharmaceutical companies and again lists of companies and their contact details were found on the internet. We contacted one which manufactures nicotine patches and asked for information on success rates.

The local telephone directory gave us names and phone numbers of therapists. We asked them for information on techniques they use and their success rates. We also asked them to refer us to others who might have been able to provide useful information. We could also have contacted the governing bodies for the various therapies.

For case studies we began with personal contacts we knew who had tried to give up smoking – both those who had been successful and those who hadn't. If you find you don't have enough case studies for your articles, send a press release to your local newspaper asking for people to contact you with their stories.

Exercises
- *Plan the research for your article.*
- *Do the research for your article.*

10 THINGS TO REMEMBER

1 *Primary sources for research are the originals – documents or eyewitnesses.*

2 *Secondary sources are 'one removed' from the event – reports, or people who heard about it.*

3 *Always try to cross-check information.*

4 *Start research with background information.*

5 *Move on to interviews.*

6 *Have more than one source for corroboration.*

7 *If sources disagree, then mention both to avoid bias.*

8 *Never quote from work that is in copyright without permission.*

9 *Press officers may have their own agendas.*

10 *Try to get information from organizations which have different agendas.*

10

Interviews and interview technique

In this chapter you will learn:
* *about the different types of interview*
* *how to prepare for an interview*
* *how to conduct an interview.*

> *Realize how far ahead mags work. Big glossy ones usually work about three months in advance. So look forward four to five months and suggest something timely for then: not an interesting issue about something that's happening right now.*
> Katy Bravery, Deputy Editor, *Saga Magazine*

Interviews and how you use the information fall into two categories:

1 *The interview is part of the research for an article, where you might talk to an expert to get facts (for example, interviewing a doctor for a medical article) or an involved person to get opinions (for example, interviewing someone who lives near the site of a proposed mobile phone mast).*

2 *The interview forms the entire article, either because the person is famous or because there is something unique and newsworthy about them.*

This chapter covers the first sort of interview, and the second sort is covered in Chapter 20.

Not all features or articles require you to interview anyone. If you are writing about your own experiences or personal expertise, it is unlikely you will need input from anyone else. But if you are relying on other people for information then you will have to interview them. Interviews add colour and human interest to a piece – the drier the topic, the more you need interviews.

Insight

Asking for, and carrying out, an interview can be daunting if you have never done one before, but if you act professionally and have your notes and questions ready, no one will know it is your first interview.

Interviews can be done on the phone, by emails or face to face. They can be a short call to get some background information or a quote, or they can be an in-depth questioning.

The agenda

Writing articles, whether they are about people or whether they use information from people, is a two-way transaction. Undoubtedly the writer gains something from the interview and the subsequent article, but the interviewee also gains from the process as well.

If they are famous, either nationally or locally, they will probably welcome the chance to have their viewpoint put in print. If they have expert knowledge they will probably want to share it with you and the public. And if they have a bone to pick, then they will welcome the chance to get it off their chest.

Most interviewees are not paid (the exception is when publications pay for exclusive rights to someone's story). People have different reasons for agreeing to be interviewed and you should always ask yourself what they expect to get out of it.

Members of the public may see the interview as a chance to put their case without understanding that the journalist has to be even-handed, and in controversial situations will have to put both points of view across. The secret is to be scrupulously fair to both sides and not slant the article one way or the other.

Off-the-record

Some interviews will be off-the-record, because for whatever reason the interviewee can't be identified. You should always respect this. Be careful how you use the information. The person might still be identifiable if you call them 'a family member who lives nearby' – there may be only one family member who lives nearby. Also, the wrong person may be thought to be the source, causing trouble for someone entirely innocent.

Before the interview

Before you pick up the phone or meet someone take time to prepare. There are several aspects to conducting a fruitful interview, and the following should be considered in advance:

▶ *setting up an interview*
▶ *phone, email or face to face*
▶ *preparing questions.*

SETTING UP AN INTERVIEW

This is the first point of contact between you and your interviewee – if you get it wrong you may not get a second bite of the cherry. Be professional, be friendly, be clear why you are contacting them and don't waffle. Some people are flattered to be asked for an interview, others find it daunting – if you suspect that your interviewee is the latter, then just talk to them until they relax.

It is important to establish quickly whether the interviewee wants to be formal and addressed by their full title or whether they prefer to be informal and use Christian names. If in doubt, err on the side of formality and then assess how the interviewee wants to proceed. It is also important to pronounce the person's name correctly.

Depending on the person being interviewed you can telephone, email or write asking for an appointment. If writing or emailing, attach your CV (see Chapter 6). Which ever method you choose you will need to explain:

▶ *who you are*
▶ *why you want this information*
▶ *what the article is about*
▶ *which type of publication it is aimed at (unless you have been specifically commissioned by a magazine do not use their name to gain access to someone)*
▶ *how long the interview will take (always ask the interviewee how long they'll be able to give you).*

If you just want a quick chat with someone who can give you a quote or some background information then ring them up, and check if they have the information you want. If they are too busy to talk at that moment, agree a time when you can ring back, and be sure to ring back at that time.

Emails are quicker than writing a letter, and are probably easier for the first-time interviewer who might be nervous about making a phone call, but remember not everyone checks their emails on a daily basis.

People who are in the public eye or who lead busy lives will need advance warning. Write to them and be prepared to wait until they can slot you into their diary.

PHONE, EMAIL OR FACE TO FACE

The choice will depend on several factors:

- ▶ *the amount and type of information needed*
- ▶ *the geographical distance between interviewer and interviewee*
- ▶ *what the interviewee prefers.*

If you only require a small amount of information then it would be a waste of time, for both you and the interviewee, to insist on a face to face meeting. This can be done via the phone or email.

> **Insight**
>
> Be careful what you say in emails – they are neither private nor secure and can easily be forwarded to a third party.

If you live a long way away from the interviewee, it is perfectly possible to carry out an in-depth interview on the phone or by email. Phone calls, which should be done at your expense, can give you a better idea of the interviewee's real thoughts and feelings, than an email. The downside is that you will have to take notes on the phone or use a recording device and then transcribe, whereas the information in an email can be slotted straight into your piece with a bit of editing.

> **Insight**
>
> It is perfectly legal to record a phone call in which you are involved and there are simple voice recorders available for this. You must however tell the person you are talking to that they are being recorded.

However, a face to face interview gives the best insight into the interviewee's take on life because as well as listening to their words you can watch their body language. If this is important, then make the effort to meet them in person.

When setting up an interview, be aware that your initial phone call may meet with the response 'Yes, let's do it now', so be ready with your questions just in case this happens.

PREPARING QUESTIONS

Do as much research as possible before the interview to establish the type of information you want from the interviewee. It helps to have a good memory. Try to hold at least the main facts about the interviewee in your head. However, in the hurry to get to the meat of the interview, it is sometimes easy to forget the basic questions such as:

- *the interviewee's full name, correctly spelt*
- *their correct title and what they want to be called in the article*
- *where they live*
- *if relevant, their age*
- *their qualifications*
- *their correct job title*
- *further contact details for them, such as business or mobile phone numbers.*

Types of question

Depending on the type of information you are looking for questions can be:

- *closed*
- *open*
- *confrontational*
- *awkward.*

CLOSED QUESTIONS

These are helpful for checking facts and figures quickly as they only need a 'Yes' or 'No' answer. For example, 'Was the mast put up in 2001?'

OPEN QUESTIONS

These encourage your interviewee to open up and express an opinion. For example, 'What effect do you think the phone mast is having on people living near it?'

CONFRONTATIONAL QUESTIONS

These are usually put to public figures, businessmen or those in high places when you are hoping for a good off-the-cuff response. However, take care when asking these types of questions because if you are too confrontational they might refuse to answer altogether. For example, 'Were you aware of research into health hazards before you built the mast?'

AWKWARD QUESTIONS

In some circumstances, there will be one or more awkward questions that you suspect the interviewee won't want to answer. How you approach this will be a matter of judgement on the day. It might be better to make these the last questions in the interview or you could find it terminated before you have started. An example of an awkward question might be, 'How much money are you being paid to site the mast on your property?'

Possible approaches to this might be to discuss the economics of running the property and to mention how useful mobile phones are.

Asking for quotes

If somebody says something particularly contentious, ask if you can quote them. They may want to reword what they've said, or be particularly anxious that you've understood exactly what they've said.

Conducting the interview

FACE TO FACE

Interviews can be anywhere: the interviewee's home, their place of work, on the hoof. Try to avoid crowded public places such as restaurants and pubs, where it is difficult to hear and where there are too many distractions. Be sure to arrive on time, with your notes properly organized.

Insight

If you are recording a face to face interview, always check your equipment beforehand, fit fresh batteries and carry spares. Never rely entirely on a recorder, carry a notebook as well.

You'll probably feel nervous during your first few interviews. Bear in mind that many people hold journalists in awe and will be even more nervous than you are. Don't rush the first few minutes, take time to get yourself settled and arrange your notes. Ask your interviewee if they are comfortable.

Insight

If you feel nervous about the interview, practise calm, slow breathing beforehand – it well help to dispel your nerves. The simplest technique is to count slowly as you breathe, four 'in' and four 'out'. If you are very nervous, try four 'in' and eight 'out'.

Pay attention to the interviewee's body language, eye contact and tone of voice. If they are struggling with something that is difficult for them to talk about, give them time and show that you are sympathetic. Although you will have your list of questions, be prepared to be flexible.

ON THE PHONE

Have your list of questions ready and make sure that you won't be disturbed for the duration of the interview. If you are planning to do a lot of phone interviews, it might be a good idea to invest in a phone headset so that you have both hands free to take notes or type directly onto the computer.

People vary in how comfortable they are on the phone. As with face to face interviewing, don't rush the first few minutes, allow your interviewee to settle down. You have far fewer cues than in a face to face interview, so listen intently.

RECORDING AN INTERVIEW

You can take written notes, or use a recorder. With written notes you may find it hard to focus on the interviewee as your attention will be on your notebook. If you are recording, you must do so openly. Recorders don't pick up sound well in noisy places, so in those circumstances you will have to take notes. Accuracy is important, so even if you are recording take a notebook to record spellings of names and technical terms.

LISTENING SKILLS

These are important, whether you are interviewing face to face or on the phone. You need to achieve a balance between allowing the interviewee time to express what they need to say, and giving them feedback that encourages them to open up. If you overdo the feedback and talk too much they will close down and be less forthcoming. Of course, you don't want them to ramble, or talk off the subject and you may need to gently bring them back to the point.

In a face to face interview, sit facing the interviewee and try not to fidget. As they talk, nod your head, and make little remarks like 'I see' or even 'Mmm'. This shows you are listening and encourages them to continue.

On the phone, you only have sound so it is important for your interviewee to know that you are paying attention. Don't rush to fill every pause, but do say something so that they know you are still there.

In the interview you should:

- *focus your attention on the speaker, not yourself*
- *not spend the time thinking about your next question while the interviewee is speaking*
- *maintain eye contact*
- *stay neutral and non-judgemental*
- *keep your body language relaxed and neutral*
- *encourage the speaker with your facial expressions and encouraging words*
- *(on the phone) not rush to fill every pause, but do say something so that they know you are paying attention.*

There are three elements to any spoken communication:

- *content*
- *voice*
- *body language.*

Content

This includes vocabulary and phrasing as well as the meaning of their words. This is important if your written piece is going to capture the flavour of the interviewee's speech and, it follows, their personality.

Voice

This is the speaker's tone, volume, speed and pitch. All of these can change and give you clues as to whether you have hit on a sensitive issue, or whether your interviewee is being less than honest or putting a spin on something.

Body language

This can be the biggest clue to the truth of what you are being told or the underlying feelings behind a statement. Understanding an individual's body language can take a long time, but some behaviours are common to most of us. Playing with your hair reveals insecurity or nervousness and folding your arms shows you are putting up a barrier.

Ending the interview

At the end of the interview ask the interviewee if you can contact them later in case you need to double-check any facts and figures. Also ask if they can give you any further contacts, then thank them and leave (or hang up). If an interview has been on a very technical and difficult subject, you could ask the interviewee if they would be willing to check the copy, but otherwise try to avoid giving copy approval.

If the interviewee insists on copy approval you will have to make a judgement, particularly if they say you can't use the information unless they have copy approval. There is of course a difference between the interviewee just checking the copy for accuracy and wanting to make major changes. If it is the latter, then your journalistic integrity is being called into question and you may choose to refuse.

DOOR KNOBBING

Stay mentally alert as the interview ends. A common behaviour – known as 'door knobbing' – means that people will often say something very important just as they are leaving, with their hand on the door knob. Doctors and counsellors are particularly aware of this. It works the same way in interviews; the interviewee might give you the most important information just as you are leaving, or ending the phone call, so be prepared.

After the interview

Immediately after the interview you need to make a note of your first impressions, so try to leave some free time, don't book yourself to do something else. Write up your notes properly as soon as possible, while everything is still fresh in your mind. If you have made a recording you don't have to transcribe every word, but go through the recording and pick out those parts that you intend to use.

Exercises
- ▶ *Set up the interview(s) for your article.*
- ▶ *Prepare the questions.*
- ▶ *Conduct the interview(s).*
- ▶ *Write up the interview(s).*

10 THINGS TO REMEMBER

1 *Interviews for background research can also be used to add human interest.*

2 *Good preparation will help you feel less nervous.*

3 *Interviews can be via phone, email or face to face.*

4 *If the interview is off-the-record, be careful that nothing reveals the interviewee's identity.*

5 *Have your questions ready before you phone for an appointment in case the interview happens on the spot.*

6 *You may have to wait for an appointment in order to see a busy person.*

7 *Face to face interviews give you the best insight because you will see body language.*

8 *Think carefully about how to approach awkward questions.*

9 *Use good listening skills.*

10 *Make notes during and immediately after the interview, while it is fresh in your mind.*

Part two

Writing an article

11

Organizing an article

In this chapter you will learn:
- *how to plan an article*
- *about different types of title*
- *about different types of order*
- *about extras.*

> *In terms of writing I look for structured, concise information which sticks to the subject and is delivered in a personal and friendly manner with some humour and wit. We are not just trying to inform readers, we are trying to interest and entertain them.*
>
> Tim Rumball, Editor, *Amateur Gardening* magazine

Planning

Once you have done the research, it is time to plan the article. Throughout this process you need to keep a clear focus on what type of article you are intending to write, because that will determine how you use your research. A celebrity interview might contain very few facts and figures, but might benefit from a fact box about the subject's life and work to one side, whereas an informative article might need the facts and figures incorporated into the main body of the text.

Start by making a list of all the different types of information you have: interviews, facts and figures, arguments for and against and so on. You'll probably have handwritten notes and computer files, and possibly tape recordings as well, so an overview will help you feel in control of the mass of information.

Decide what information is absolutely essential to the article, what should be included if possible, and what is best left out. Remind yourself once more exactly what you intend to achieve with this particular article, and be ruthless in excluding anything that doesn't contribute to that aim.

If the brief for the article was very specific, then your research should have been very focused. However, writers often have to do a certain amount of digging into a subject before they can be sure of the approach they want to take, so that the list of research could contain all sorts of irrelevant items; this is an increasing problem due to the wealth of information on the internet.

Insight

If you have trouble deciding what is essential to the article think in terms of 'Yes' 'No' and 'Maybe', create a chart with those three headings and enter items accordingly.

Work in progress

Our article was commissioned by a magazine with a largely middle-aged readership, many of whom are smokers who would like to quit. The brief was to look into giving up smoking, and the tone of the magazine is generally upbeat. Many different articles could be produced from the information discovered during our research but we decided to focus on the positive benefits of quitting, and the ways of achieving this.

Our research gave us information on the following:

1   *statistics on smoking-related deaths*
2   *statistics on the cost to the health service of treating smoking related illnesses*
3   *statistics on the value to the economy of the tobacco industry*
4   *statistics on smoking in Third World countries*
5   *information on harmful ingredients in tobacco smoke*
6   *information about the law on smoking in public places*
7   *interview with a doctor*
8   *interview with a lung cancer patient*
9   *interviews with teenage smokers*
10   *interviews with smokers, both those who have succeeded and those who have failed in giving up*
11   *addresses of websites that aim to help smokers give up*
12   *press releases relating to products that aim to help smokers give up*
13   *information about using hypnosis and alternative therapies to quit smoking.*

In other words, the article must use items 9, 10, 11 and 12. Items 3, 4, 5, 7 and 8, while interesting in themselves, are not relevant to the main thrust of this particular article. The statistics from items 1, 2 and 5 will be useful to supplement the main article. Finally, item 6, the interview with a doctor, should be useful in part.

Note that there is plenty of material in this body of research for other articles: a hard-hitting one for a teenage magazine about the dangers of smoking, or a 'Triumph Over Tragedy' piece about the lung cancer patient. A little more research could produce a campaigning article about the lives of workers in tobacco-growing countries.

A shape for the final article begins to emerge – the main body will look at smokers who have succeeded in giving up and will examine the various techniques they tried. The interviews with people who failed can be used if there is something to be learnt from their difficulties.

Reading through the notes it becomes clear that all the methods are successful but some work for some people and some for others, and so the thrust of the article will be advising people to choose a method that is most likely to suit them rather than trying to judge between the different methods. Selected quotes from the doctor can be used to focus on the medical benefits to the individual of quitting (and possibly to lay the myth that weight gain is inevitable).

Choosing a title

You already have a working title for your article – if only as a way of labelling your research – but now is a good moment to stop and think about a more permanent title. Aim for something that really captures the spirit of the piece you are intending to write, and that is appropriate for the magazine you are aiming at.

> **Insight**
>
> Choosing the title now will help you stay focused on what exactly you are trying to do. If, after writing the piece you find the title no longer relevant, check whether you have moved away from your original proposal.

It's important to understand that the piece may appear under an entirely different title. It is part of a sub editor's job to put titles on features, and they will only use yours if they think it is the best one.

First look at the magazine and see how they title pieces. Next, make a list of keywords that you think will feature in the finished article (this list will help you with the writing too). Use the list to generate different titles until you find one that works.

There are a number of different ways to arrive at a title:

▶ **the question:** *'Would you like to stop smoking?'*
▶ **the label:** *using your keywords list, construct a simple title that says what the piece is about, for example '5 easy ways to give up smoking'.*

- ▶ **the exclamation (or screamer):** *'Stop smoking now! Live ten years longer!'*
- ▶ **the quotation or saying:** *'To cease smoking is the easiest thing I ever did. I ought to know because I've done it a thousand times.' (Mark Twain) It also works well if a familiar quotation or saying is twisted in some way: 'No smoke without cigarettes'.*
- ▶ **the pun:** *like the quotation, it is often combined with a well-known phrase or saying, for example 'Baccy to the future', 'Smoke gets in your eyes (and everyone else's)', 'Packet in'.*
- ▶ **alliteration:** *where most of the words begin with the same letter or the same-sounding letter, for example 'Say no to ciggies', 'Ta-ta to tobacco', 'Farewell fags'.*

Work in progress

By a process of elimination, in this case the question, 'Would you like to stop smoking?' looks the most promising title. It may not have pizazz, but it tells the reader straight away what the article is about. The label is nearly as good. The exclamation is not suitable for the rather staid magazine in question, the Mark Twain quotation is not familiar enough to readers, the twisted saying is rather lifeless and the pun and the alliteration are too tabloid* in feel.

Deciding the order

Once you know what items you are going to use in the article, you need to decide on the order to place them in. An article needs an underlying shape to give it coherence, and the order in which you

---

*tabloid: used to describe the style of populist journalism used in the tabloid newspapers (which are half the size of the broadsheet newspapers). In fact, the broadsheets are beginning to change to tabloid size, but the term remains in use.

present the information will determine the shape. There is a range of choices available:

- ▶ **reader's interest:** *answering the questions that a reader would ask.*
- ▶ **repetition:** *a series of points that build, each one stronger than the one before.*
- ▶ **chronological:** *telling the story in the order that events happened in time.*
- ▶ **sequential:** *taking points in the correct practical order, used in 'how-to' articles.*
- ▶ **climax:** *building to a dramatic conclusion.*
- ▶ **reverse:** *starting with the conclusion followed by explanation.*
- ▶ **logical:** *such as a problem followed by its solution.*
- ▶ **news:** *newspaper articles usually start with all the most important information in the first paragraph, and then enlarge and add to this (known as a pyramid shape). Features don't usually follow this pattern but it is an option.*

If the order doesn't seem blindingly obvious then you will need to find the best way to structure the article. Look through the information that you have already chosen for the article and use it to make a list of headings showing what the article will cover. Write these headings out randomly on a large sheet of paper and underneath each one make notes about what should be included.

Work in progress

The shape of our article will be a logical sequence starting with the interviews (the problem), followed by statistics to back up why it is important to stop smoking (the reasons) and ending with successful techniques and therapies (the solution).

Fine-tuning the order

Take a moment to think about the finished article. What will be its main point? What will the reader take away from it? What will make the most interesting opening and closing paragraphs? Above all, the underlying structure of the article must be appropriate to the content.

Insight

If you're not sure which type of order to use, then go for reader's interest as it works for almost all articles. Make a list of questions that a reader might ask and put them into an order that leads from one point to the next.

Work in progress

The underlying structure of interviews with smokers who have been successful followed by techniques and therapies, is entirely suitable for an article which is to show the readers it is possible to kick the habit. A structure that emphasises the grim death rates among smokers might not encourage them in the same way as success stories and could turn them off entirely from reading the article.

The article will work best with a reader's interest order. The key will be in writing up the interviews in such a way that every reader will find someone to identify with. So our basic order could be:

▶ **introduction:** *the personal experience of the writer*
▶ **body copy:** *interviews with smokers*
▶ **ending:** *a positive affirmation that it can be done.*

A feature will always be a mixture of opinion, fact, anecdote,
quotes and argument, but some facts will clearly be difficult to
incorporate, and stodgy chunks of information can easily break up
the flow of the writing. These things can be put into the 'extras'.

Extras

If you look at almost any feature you will see that as well as the
main copy there are various other items of print on the page (see
Chapter 4 'Page furniture'). These are the extras and they have a
range of functions. Some are provided by the author of the article,
either from their own research or from press releases and public
relations officers. Others will be added by the sub editor if they
think the article needs it, for example, an explanation of a technical
matter that the sub will request from an expert.

The most important thing about these extras is that they should
be easy to read – this is not a place for you to show off your
authorial pyrotechnics.

Extras can be used in various ways:

▶ **pre-set information:** *a series of pre-set headings with relevant
information under each one. This is commonly used for
regular reviews such as in motoring magazines for describing
the features of a new car or in travel magazines for describing
the merits of a holiday destination. The reader knows exactly
what to expect and can access the information, and make
comparisons, quickly and easily.*
▶ **added value:** *this is the information supplied by other writers
or experts.*

- ▶ **speed-read summary:** *a box with the key points of the article summarized, often with bullet points. Aimed at people who are too busy to read the whole article.*
- ▶ **statistics:** *rather than struggle to write up continuous sentences, show statistics under headings or in a table. They are more readable this way and more easily absorbed.*
- ▶ **advice:** *use for tips about the subject of the article or for product comparisons.*
- ▶ **case studies**
- ▶ **stories**

Work in progress

Our article needs the following extras:

- ▶ *quit-smoking website addresses in a box*
- ▶ *brief information about products mentioned in the interviews in another box*
- ▶ *separate panel with a factual explanation of alternative therapies including hypnosis.*

Final check

By now you have a good idea of what the final article is going to be like, and this is a good moment to step back and check that it is going to fulfil the brief and be suitable for the magazine.

Work in progress

The obvious flaw with our smoking article is that there may not be anything of interest in it for people who have

(Contd)

never smoked (it's reasonable to assume that readers who have smoked in the past will always have an interest in the subject). If it is appropriate for the magazine, the writer could add a quiz, the aim of which is for the reader to be able work out from the answers which method of quitting would suit them best. Even non-smokers are likely to enjoy a quiz that tells them something about their personality.

Exercises
▶ *Plan the article.*
▶ *Organize the information.*
▶ *Make a list of possible titles.*
▶ *Decide on the order of points.*
▶ *Decide on the extras, if any.*

10 THINGS TO REMEMBER

1 *Always spend time planning an article before you begin to write.*

2 *Decide if the research is central to the article.*

3 *List all the different types of information you have.*

4 *Decide what is essential and what can be left out.*

5 *Choose a title that is right for the article and for the magazine.*

6 *Decide on the order for items.*

7 *Decide on the underlying shape for the article.*

8 *Fine-tune to ensure good opening and closing paragraphs.*

9 *Decide what will go in the 'extras'.*

10 *Do a final check to make sure the article will meet the brief.*

12

Basic writing skills

In this chapter you will learn:
- *to write simple sentences*
- *to write short, focused paragraphs*
- *to use accurate punctuation.*

> *English is a very rich language, and a good writer will search for just the right words to convey their meaning. Anything less and the writing will be sloppy and unconvincing.*
>
> Jan Barwick, Editor, *Devon Life*

Once you have organized the material, you will be keen to start writing the article. Journalism isn't rocket science, but writing clearly and effectively is more difficult than many of us realize.

While sub editors will be prepared to correct the odd spelling mistake or grammatical error, they will not rewrite a badly written article. So to ensure that yours has the best possible chance of being used you should pay due attention to grammar, spelling and punctuation.

We have included some basic information about grammar and punctuation, but for a more detailed explanation use a good grammar book or check on the websites listed in Appendix B.

Grammar and idiom

The conventions of grammar change over time but a journalist must follow what is currently believed to be correct. However, grammar often appears to impose rules on language that speakers of the language resist using. When the resistance triumphs, then idioms develop. In other words, idioms are ways of using language that have grown to be accepted even though they may not be grammatically correct, or may not make logical sense. For example:

> *'He's never had a job that I know of.'*

> *'That I know of is an idiom and this sentence, to be grammatically correct, should read: 'He's never had a job as far as I am aware.'*

Speech is always highly idiomatic, and some forms of writing, such as scientific reports, should not use idiom at all. Journalists can, and should, use idiom as it makes their writing more naturalistic and accessible.

Insight

Model your grammar, use of idiom and punctuation on the magazine you are writing for.

SENTENCES

A sentence is a group of words which can stand alone and be understood. There are simple and compound sentences, but in journalistic writing it is more common to use short, simple sentences. This is where analysing magazine articles proves its value. In news writing the first word of the sentence is the most important. In magazine writing it still carries a lot of weight but the last word is also important.

PARAGRAPHS

Paragraphs are made up from one or more sentences which all relate to one topic or theme. Ideally each paragraph should have a key sentence which sums up what the theme of the paragraph is about. Usually it is the first sentence but it does not have to be. The rest of the sentences amplify or add evidence to the topic or theme.

The following paragraph from a review of a small caravan is messy because it doesn't follow the natural order of things and there is no key sentence:

> *'Making up the bed is simply a question of pulling out the board from under the settee and adding the infill cushions that are stored in the wardrobe, but when it is done you can't open the fridge to get the milk for your morning cuppa. The bed is comfortable enough but not over long and there is no reading light. The best place to store the bedding is in the underseat locker.'*

Let's rewrite it and look at the rewrite sentence by sentence:

> *'Many caravanners dread the moment when they have to make up the bed, but the manufacturers have made life simple. Retrieve the duvet, which is best stored in the underseat locker. Then simply pull out the board from under the settee and add the infill cushions that are stored in the wardrobe. The bed is comfortable enough but not over long, and there is no reading light.'*

Analysis
> *'Many caravanners dread the moment when they have to make up the bed but the manufacturers have made life simple.'*

This is the key sentence that tells the reader this paragraph will be about sleeping arrangements and that they are going to be good.

The following sentences add further information to the topic in a chronological order.

> *'Retrieve the duvet, which is best stored in the underseat locker.'*

The first step is to retrieve the duvet.

> *'Then simply pull out the board from under the settee and add the infill cushions that are stored in the wardrobe.'*

The second step is to make up the bed.

> *'The bed is comfortable enough but not over long, and there is no reading light.'*

Having learned how to make up the bed the reader wants to know what it's like in use.

In the original draft the words 'but when it is done you can't open the fridge to get the milk for your morning cuppa', do not conform to the theme or topic, so are rewritten to start the next paragraph:

> *'Come the morning, however, there is a major drawback in that the foot of the bed blocks the fridge, so you can't get to the milk for a morning cuppa in bed.'*

Spelling

We all know that English spelling is illogical, complicated and nightmarishly difficult to learn. Computer spellcheckers can certainly help with some of the problems, but remember to set yours to either US English or UK English, depending on which market you are writing for.

The big weakness of spellcheckers is that they will never pick up on a spelling mistake that is also a word, leading to such howlers as:

> *'Joan of Arc was burnt at the steak.' (Should be 'stake'.)*

> *'He gave me the bear facts.' (Should be 'bare'.)*

All you can do, if your spelling is this bad, is buy a pocket dictionary and refer to it constantly. Your spelling will improve gradually and, in the meantime, you must hope for an eagle-eyed sub editor to save you from embarrassing yourself.

Punctuation

COMMAS

Commas are used to give structure to sentences and can also have an effect on meaning:

> *'Ann is, obviously, happy to help.'*

This suggests that the speaker has no doubt about Ann's willingness to help.

> *'Ann is obviously happy to help.'*

Without commas the sentence suggests that Ann's happiness is there for all to see.

Most commas, however, are there for stylistic reasons. Fashions change and how many you use will depend on what you've been taught and the house style.

SEMICOLONS

Semicolons are rarely used in magazine writing because the general rule is to use short sentences.

COLONS

Colons are placed before an explanation or list.

QUOTATION MARKS

These are also known as quotes, speech marks or inverted commas. Anything in quotation marks is understood by the reader to be either the actual words of the person being interviewed or a passage taken directly from a book or document. Remember that this applies to headlines as well as body text.

Quotation marks are used to enclose direct speech. If the remark is a sentence, then put a full stop inside the quotation marks. If the remark is just a phrase, put the full stop outside the quotation marks. For example:

> *'I'm not going to be beaten,' Greg told me, 'I'm going to fight until I get my pension.' Or:*

> *Greg is not going to be beaten. As he said, he is going to 'fight 'til his last breath'.*

House style will dictate whether to use single quotation marks ('Hello') or double quotation marks ("Hello") round a speech. Whichever it is, use the opposite for quotes within quotes:

> *'I asked her,' he said, 'and she said "get lost".' Or:*

> *"I asked her," he said, "and she said 'get lost'."*

Very common short quotes from well-known writers or the Bible don't need quote marks, for example:

> *At first glance it seems that Greg is hoist with his own petard.*

When using passages from something written by someone else remember that there are limits to how much you can quote (see Chapter 9).

Finally, don't fall into the common trap of using quotation marks to mark out a word that you're not too sure about, maybe because it feels slangy or foreign. For example, don't write:

Gary is a bit of a 'dude' or

Ideas can come to us from the 'zeitgeist'.

If you are unsure of a word, don't use it.

APOSTROPHES

Apostrophes are tiny marks on the page, and yet they probably cause more problems than the rest of punctuation put together. The basic rules of using apostrophes are quite simple.

1 *An apostrophe shows that something has been left out of a word:*

   can't = cannot

   hasn't = has not.

2 *Don't use an apostrophe to show that a word has been shortened; either use the whole word or use the abbreviation without an apostrophe:*

   through not thru'

   phone not 'phone.

3 *An apostrophe shows possession:*

   John's car = the car belonging to John.

4 *It helps some people to think of possession as also showing that something has been left out: John's car = the car of John.*

Possession or plural?

In English most plurals are created by adding an 's' to a word, and possession is shown by adding an apostrophe and an 's'. Confusion over this leads to most of the mistakes with apostrophes. Don't panic, take one step at a time and you will be able to work out what is needed.

▶ *A singular word has no 's' and no apostrophe: one cat.*
▶ *A singular word with a possessive has an apostrophe followed by 's': one cat's pyjamas.*
▶ *A plural word has an 's' and no apostrophe: six cats.*
▶ *A plural word with a possessive has an 's' followed by an apostrophe: six cats' pyjamas.*

There are three further things to understand.

1 *Some words end in 's', particularly names. There is no hard and fast rule for how to show possession with these words, but a good guide is to say the word out loud and then punctuate accordingly:*

   William Morris's pony

   Jesus' disciples

2 *If you're not comfortable with the result, restructure the sentence and use 'of' or 'belonging to':*

   The pony belonging to William Morris

3 *Some plurals are not formed by adding an 's'. To show possession for these words use an apostrophe followed by an 's':*

   Children's books

   Sheep's eyeballs

4   *Time is also possessive:*

   In one year's time I shall be nine.

5   *The same rules of singular and plural apply in this situation as well:*

   In ten years' time I shall be 18.

'Its' or 'it's'?

Writing quickly it is easy to make a mistake and confuse 'its' and 'it's', so always check your final draft for this simple error. 'It's' is an abbreviated form of 'it is' or 'it has'. 'Its' is a word used to denote possession of something but it doesn't need an apostrophe because it is a complete word and nothing has been taken out of it. It is a pronoun in the same way as 'mine', 'yours', 'ours' and so on. For example:

   It's a lovely day = it is a lovely day.

   The dog licked its paw = the dog licked the paw belonging to itself.

Insight

If you really can't decide where to put the apostrophe then leave it out; fewer readers will notice a missed one than a wrongly inserted one.

DASHES

Using dashes instead of colons and semicolons gives writing a racier more colloquial feel, but don't go overboard with them. For most readers a dash in the middle of a sentence suggests that what follows will be unexpected or surprising in some way, for example:

   Beautician Alice Smith says there are 30 ways to look younger – but why would you want to?

See below for using dashes as parenthesis.

ELLIPSIS

An ellipsis is a row of three dots used to show that something has been omitted from a written quotation, for example:

> *In* Get Your Articles Published *the authors state that 'using dashes... gives writing a racier, more colloquial feel'.*

This means you are using only those parts of a quote that are relevant, although you shouldn't use this to distort the writer's meaning:

> *In* Get Your Articles Published *the authors state that 'For most readers a dash... will be unexpected'.*

You don't need to use an ellipsis when omitting something from a spoken quote. Never use more than three dots.

EXCLAMATION MARKS

Known in the trade as 'screamers', these are to be avoided except in headlines. Some writers develop the habit of using them to signal a joke or light-hearted remark:

> *I fell downstairs, twisted my ankle, dropped all my shopping and broke my mobile phone. It just wasn't my day!*

They are also used to signal to the reader that a remark is not meant to be taken seriously:

> *My son came home covered in mud. I could have cheerfully strangled him!*

If they've become habitual for you, your writing may look bare without them but both of these uses are to be avoided.

> **Insight**
> Break the habit of popping exclamation marks into your
> everyday writing and you will soon learn to do without them
> in journalism too.

PARENTHESIS

A parenthesis is a piece of information inserted into a sentence or
paragraph that already makes sense without it. There are different
ways of doing this. The simplest is with commas:

> *Gary's dog, Rover, goes everywhere with him.*

> *Gary's dog, given to him by a charity, goes everywhere
> with him.*

Round brackets are, confusingly, also known as parentheses.
Use them to give an abbreviation or to make a clearer separation
between the main sentence and the extra information:

> *The Author's Licensing and Collecting Society (ALCS) was set
> up to collect payments due to writers.*

> *The Author's Licensing and Collecting Society (set up to
> collect payments due to writers) is usually known as ALCS.*

Very strong parenthesis can be marked with dashes:

> *June is a feisty woman – she flares up at the least mention
> of plastic surgery – and she hasn't let her scars stop her from
> enjoying life.*

Square brackets have a conventional use to denote anything that
the writer or editor has added to a quote or reported speech as
an explanation. This can be extra information or something that
makes the sense of the quote clearer:

> *Greg said 'I'm going to take this to the Minister [John Smith]
> and see what he has to say for himself.'*

Square brackets with 'sic' (a Latin word meaning 'thus' or 'so') denotes that the writer knows there is an error in the quote, and that they've chosen to leave it in. It can also indicate the writer's surprise or disbelief in what they are quoting – this use can suggest that the writer is being too clever by half:

> *June told me what she really liked was a nice romantical [sic] evening out.*

Exercise
▶ *Re-analyse the magazine articles you have been looking at and check for the correct usage of apostrophes.*

10 THINGS TO REMEMBER

1 *Aim to write clearly and effectively.*

2 *Pay attention to grammar, spelling and punctuation.*

3 *Follow the currently accepted usages.*

4 *Use short direct sentences.*

5 *Give each paragraph a key sentence.*

6 *Use a spellchecker but don't rely on it completely.*

7 *Keep punctuation simple.*

8 *Get your head round the apostrophe rules.*

9 *A lack of commas can affect the meaning of the sentence.*

10 *Use exclamation marks sparsely.*

13

....

More about writing

In this chapter you will learn:
* *some basic rules of journalism*
* *how to handle factual information*
* *some journalistic conventions.*

> *Good writing isn't flowery writing. Make sure that everything you write says exactly what you want it to say. If it's not clear, then rewrite it.*
>
> Jan Barwick, Editor, *Devon Life*

Magazine writing has much in common with news journalism. All journalism is ephemeral – it is not expected to survive in the way that books do, and journalistic writing reflects that. It is informal, easy to read, accessible and reflects current language usage.

....

Insight

Be particularly careful writing your opening paragraph – if it is overly complicated your readers will quickly lose interest.

....

_____

Basics

The basic rule of journalistic writing is to let the message come through. George Orwell called this prose 'like a windowpane', meaning that the reader should not be aware of your stylistic writing tricks, but should look through them to the content.

In fact many people including Orwell have tried to define what makes good journalistic writing, with various lists of rules. However, they can all be reduced to two basic rules:

1 *Make your meaning clear.*
2 *Make life easy for the reader.*

From these we can derive a set of suggestions that in most cases will lead to maximum clarity and ease of reading. They should not be regarded as absolute rules because each one of them can be broken if the circumstances demand it. These are the principles to keep in mind:

▶ *use short words*
▶ *use concrete words*
▶ *use active verbs*
▶ *use positive statements*
▶ *avoid special vocabularies*
▶ *avoid cliché*
▶ *avoid ambiguity*
▶ *avoid empty words*
▶ *write with economy*
▶ *write simply*
▶ *be precise*
▶ *write as you speak.*

USE SHORT WORDS

Short words that convey your meaning accurately will always be more easily understood than longer equivalents, for example: 'conjuring' not 'prestidigitation'. In English this usually means that you will use the Anglo-Saxon word in preference to the Latin, for example: use 'rough' not 'unrefined'. It will often mean that two short words are better than one long one, for example: use 'Best wishes' not 'Felicitations'.

However, the richness of the English vocabulary means that each of the available words will have acquired slightly different meanings over time. Don't hesitate to drop 'dirty' in favour of 'sullied' if you need the suggestion of contamination as well as filth that this conveys.

USE CONCRETE WORDS

Readers understand concrete words much more easily than abstract. This doesn't mean that you should avoid abstract concepts, only that you should write about them with an accessible vocabulary. For example:

> *In economics, the law of diminishing returns is said to apply when one of the factors of production is held fixed in supply. Successive additions of the other factors will lead to an increase in returns up to a point, but beyond this point returns will diminish.*

Both the grammar and the vocabulary of this explanation make it tedious and difficult to follow – magazine readers shouldn't need to pass an economics exam. However, you may need to explain diminishing returns as part of an article. For example:

> *Imagine you have never tasted chocolate. Your first chocolate will taste wonderful. So will the next one. And the next. But eventually the buzz will wear off. That is diminishing returns.*

USE ACTIVE VERBS

Active verbs have a dynamism which takes the reader into the heart of the action. Active verbs are more straightforward than passive verbs. Readers will always grasp the meaning of an active sentence more quickly and easily than a passive one, for example:

Active: *The man snatched the woman's handbag.*

Passive: *The woman's handbag was snatched by the man.*

The first sentence is easy to read and has an order that feels natural in English – it starts with the subject ('the man') moves on to the action ('snatched') and ends with the object of the action ('the woman's handbag'). The passive version feels complicated and is longer by two words.

Incomplete passives are particularly irritating for the reader:

The woman's handbag was snatched.

This immediately gives the reader a feeling of withheld information and an unanswered question: Who snatched the handbag? If this is the effect you want, then use an incomplete passive, but use it sparingly.

Sometimes an incomplete passive is useful when you have a quote that you can't attribute:

It was claimed that the handbag was empty.

Occasionally a passive statement is useful precisely because it changes the word order and throws the emphasis onto a different aspect of the information. In journalism the first word of the sentence alerts the reader to what the main thrust of the sentence will be and the passive form allows you to vary the first word. For example:

An intruder snatched the Queen's handbag.

The Queen's handbag was snatched by an intruder.

Here is it clearly important to mention the name of the victim as early as possible, therefore the second example is better.

Equally, the passive can allow you to delay an important piece of information until the end of the sentence and achieve surprise or emphasis:

The woman's handbag was snatched by a large, hairy, tattooed poodle.

USE POSITIVE STATEMENTS

This doesn't mean that you should only say positive things, but that you should look for the positive way of expressing an idea. For example:

> use 'Christmas is a bad time to be a turkey'
>
> not 'Christmas is not a good time to be a turkey'.

The exception to this is when you want the extra emphasis of using 'not'. This can be coupled with repetition for greater effect:

> Christmas is not a good time to paint the ceiling, not a good time to run out of sellotape, and definitely not a good time to be a turkey.

AVOID SPECIAL VOCABULARIES

This relates to jargon, scientific and technical terms and foreign phrases that are not in everyday use. Where possible, always try to find an everyday equivalent and use that word instead. If special words are unavoidable, then find a way to explain them. Explanations can be inserted in brackets after the first use of the word or, if this looks too clumsy and breaks up the flow, use a fact box.

Of course if you are writing for a specialized readership you can use whatever special vocabularies are appropriate for that readership.

Insight
The clue to how much specialized vocabulary you should use is in the magazine itself – check two or three recent issues to see what is acceptable.

AVOID CLICHÉ

Journalists have an uneasy relationship with cliché. They are always advised to avoid using clichés, and yet at the same time they are told to write in a way that is easy for readers to understand quickly. Images and analogies that are highly original require a degree of effort on the part of the reader; that is fine for poetry but not appropriate for journalism. Clichéd expressions on the other hand are easily understood.

In addition, the cliché is a moving target. All phrases are original at some point in time, and some become so popular that they turn into clichés. When Shakespeare wrote 'hoist with his own petard' he was, as far as we know, coining a new phrase, one that survives as a cliché at a time when very few people know what a petard is. Not many clichés have a life of over four centuries of course. At the time of writing, 'does exactly what it says on the tin' is making the journey from advertising slogan through the world of stand-up comedy into cliché, but no doubt it will disappear entirely before long.

> **Insight**
> All a writer can do is be as sensitive as possible to the changes in language and avoid using the oldest and tiredest clichés.

AVOID AMBIGUITY

English is a wonderfully subtle and flexible language but inevitably there is a price to pay for these qualities. Because you are focused on what you are trying to say and know exactly what you mean to say, it is easy to overlook the fact that the sentence can also mean something else entirely. For example, 'They are eating apples' can mean that some people are eating apples, or that the apples are eating apples, not cooking apples.

Many ambiguities are generated by the compression needed in headlines. For example, 'Teenager thrown from van in bid to foil theft' relates to a story of a teenager who jumped on a van in an attempt to stop it being stolen. However, it can also mean that someone threw the teenager out of the van in an attempt to stop someone stealing something.

The only way to be certain that your writing is not ambiguous is to check it thoroughly, and if uncertain get someone else to read it.

Ambiguities arising from grammatical confusion are harder to avoid and the little pronoun 'it' causes a lot of the trouble because it is not always clear which noun the 'it' is replacing. For example, 'She left her handbag hanging by its handle because it was wet.' In this case the 'it' could be referring to the handbag, the handle or the weather.

AVOID EMPTY WORDS

First drafts in particular are often littered with empty words and phrases that function as a writer's security blanket. Words like 'basically' and 'simply' and phrases like 'nevertheless it can be said that' can usually be deleted without any loss of meaning. Many empty phrases can be reduced to one word – 'for the purpose of' can be replaced with 'for'. Avoid saying the same thing twice: 'I myself think' just means 'I think'.

WRITE WITH ECONOMY

Good journalism has no room for waffle. If you don't have enough words to reach your target, then do some more research, or another interview, and add some more information to your article. Go through your drafts sentence by sentence and remove any superfluous words. If in doubt, cut it out.

If you use short words, short sentences and short paragraphs you will find it much easier to write with economy.

WRITE SIMPLY

Ideas and information that are simply expressed are easily understood. Many of the items in this list relate to simple vocabulary but a journalist should also try to use simple grammar. Long sentences with many subordinate clauses make it difficult for the reader to follow the sense. Look at the following example:

> *When the man, who had been released on bail pending an appeal, approached the woman, who was travelling back from a traditional Greek wedding reception and was carrying all of the bride's cash gifts in her handbag, a sum of some two thousand pounds, she became alarmed, but was unable to prevent him from snatching her handbag.*

Both the writer and reader are lost in a maze of phrases and subordinate clauses. The following simplified version is much more readable:

> *The man approached the woman and snatched her handbag. The bag contained two thousand pounds in cash, which had been given to the bride at a traditional Greek wedding. The man had been released on bail pending an appeal.*

News journalists often use strings of adjectives and adverbs to pack information into sentences:

> *The bleached-blonde overweight 47-year-old mother of five said…*

This is understandable given the time and space constraints of news, but is best avoided in magazine journalism. Use simple sentences consisting mainly of verbs and nouns and use qualifiers sparingly.

BE PRECISE

This applies to both vocabulary and grammar. Choose the words that will express exactly what you need to say, and place them in carefully and accurately composed sentences.

WRITE AS YOU SPEAK

Write as you speak is a common piece of advice to journalists, and yet it is clearly not desirable to write as most of us speak:

> *He walked right up to me, just like that, he just, I was coming down the road, I didn't even, he just walked right up to me, I was at my niece's wedding, he just came up and took my bag, he never said a word...*

And so on and so on. Even when we are not in a state of shock most of us speak in disjointed phrases with many a hesitation, deviation and repetition. Written down, speech looks ridiculous, so what can be meant by the advice to write as you speak?

As well as being rambling and ungrammatical, speech is informal, idiomatic and direct. These are the qualities that are useful to a journalist.

> Don't write: *The woman expressed great pleasure at the return of her handbag complete with banknotes and coinage.*

> Do write: *The woman was delighted to get her handbag back with the money still inside it.*

Factual information

There is a fine line to be drawn between giving too much factual information and alienating the reader and giving sufficient that everyone understands what the article is about, for example:

> *Offer up the three-pin plug to the wall socket ensuring that the larger single pin is aligned with the corresponding position in the socket. Once so aligned, apply pressure to the*

plug sufficient to engage the pins in the socket. Depress the switch on the socket (if one is fitted) and subsequently depress the 'mains power on' switch on the computer. Or

Plug the computer in and switch it on.

Of course this is exaggerated and nobody would seriously write the first example. It is reasonable to assume that readers know how to plug in an electrical item, but there are well-documented examples of users not being able to find the 'On' switch on computers (or videos or vacuum cleaners for that matter). For those people example two would be far too brief.

Conveying emotion

Emotion in an article comes from either the writer or the subject. It covers a range of feelings from excitement to anger and despair. If the writer wants to express their own emotion they will use the first person and emotive language:

Forget Alton Towers. For the ultimate white-knuckle ride you can't beat a trip with the crack RAF parachute team, the Falcons – as I was about to find out.

If the emotion comes from the subject then the article will be written in the third person:

The death of a child is a traumatic experience for any family; but to find a healthy baby lifeless in its cot is the ultimate nightmare for all parents.

The style of any article will be largely determined by the requirements of the target magazine and the brief if there is one, but there will always be choices to be made within those parameters.

Gunning Fog Index

This is a way of measuring the readability of a piece of writing. It simply measures the average number of words in a sentence and adds the percentage of words with three or more syllables. The resulting figure is the number of years of education a reader would need in order to be able to understand the piece. Clearly writing that uses short words and short sentences will have a lower score than writing that uses long words and long sentences.

A Gunning Fog Index of below ten is desirable for most journalism, although some publications have an average of slightly more than this. There is software that measures the Gunning Fog Index of writing and, although it is quite a blunt weapon, it can be a useful indicator for the beginner (see Appendix B).

Some versions of Microsoft Word will also measure the readability of writing. Click on 'Tools' then 'Spelling and Grammar', check the article sentence by sentence and at the end an information box will come up giving the statistics. The important ones are:

▶ *Words per sentence: check this against the house style of your chosen magazine.*
▶ *Passive sentences: the fewer the better.*
▶ *Flesch Reading Ease: it rates text out of 100, the higher the score the easier it is to understand the writing. Aim for between 60 and 70.*
▶ *Flesch-Kincaid Grade Level: similar to the Gunning Fog Index in that it measures the educational level of the reader. Aim for a level around 8.*

First, second or third person

You will need to decide which person the article will be written in.

FIRST PERSON

Articles that are opinion pieces or reviews should be written using 'I' or 'we'. For example, 'I thought the play was excellent' or 'I find that as I get older my sense of taste is diminishing'. The first person is also often used for 'Triumph Over Tragedy' stories, including those that are ghost written, and sometimes for interviews (see Chapter 20). These types of articles are easily accessible to the reader and pull them into the writer's world.

SECOND PERSON

The second person is used in articles where the writer is speaking directly to the reader and is telling the reader something the reader wants to know. They are written using 'you' and the form is used mainly in advice articles and sometimes used in how-to articles (see Chapter 22). For example, the article on giving up smoking could be written in the second person if the underlying structure is changed to giving advice. It might well benefit from the personal feel that 'you' gives to writing.

THIRD PERSON

Writing in the third person involves the use of 'he', 'she', 'it' or 'they'. It is the most common form of article writing.

Numbers

There are certain journalistic conventions which dictate how numbers are written. The following are the ones most commonly used, but check the house style to be on the safe side.

FIGURES

Numbers nine and under are expressed as words. Numbers 10 and over are written as figures. However, don't mix numbers and words in the same sentence:

Every day 8–12 people are diagnosed with Panic Syndrome.

The only time numbers over nine are written as words is at the beginning of a sentence:

> *Twelve people voted against the motion.*

PERCENTAGES AND FRACTIONS

For most people percentages are harder to understand than fractions, but many figures are not easily expressed as fractions.

Some publications prefer the use of the percentage sign '%', others like the words written out 'per cent'. Likewise some publications like fractions to be written '½'. Others prefer them written out 'half'. Whatever you do, never mix percentages and fractions in the same sentence. Don't write:

> *Over a half of all school children never help around the house, and 13% of those don't know how to boil an egg.*

Dates can be expressed with dashes: 1950–53. Alternatively, use 'between 1950 and 1953' or 'from 1950 to 1953'. Never use 'between... to' or 'from... and'.

Exercises
- ▶ *Analyse articles from your target magazines for:*
  - ▷ *clear writing*
  - ▷ *use of emotion.*

---

10 THINGS TO REMEMBER

1   *Make your meaning clear.*

2   *Make life easy for your reader.*

3   *Use short words, concrete words and active verbs.*

4   *Use positive statements.*

5   *Avoid special vocabularies.*

6   *Avoid cliché, ambiguity and empty words.*

7   *Don't waffle, write simply and be precise.*

8   *Give just enough factual information.*

9   *Convey emotion only where appropriate.*

10   *Decide whether to use first, second or third person.*

14

Opening and closing paragraphs

In this chapter you will learn:
- *more about structure*
- *about types of opening paragraph*
- *about types of ending.*

> *Ideally you need to grab the reader with the very first sentence, to intrigue them and to make them want to read on. If the first sentence is tedious, or too lengthy, they won't.*
>
> Jan Barwick, Editor, *Devon Life*

The basic structure of all magazine articles is beginning, middle and end. Almost always this will mean introduction, main body and conclusion, but occasionally you might decide to plunge straight in without an introductory paragraph, or to start with a conclusion and use the article to explain how it was reached (this would work, for instance, if the conclusion were something shocking).

If you have worked through the steps in the previous chapters you should have a good idea of how you want to write the first draft. Concentrate on expressing the ideas clearly and coherently as explained in Chapter 11. Try to write it in the style that is appropriate for the chosen magazine, but focus on content to start with.

Of course, you can write it without doing any planning, but you will need to allow extra time for editing if you do it that way.

This chapter will focus on the opening and closing paragraphs. It may seem strange to lump the two together, but like two bookends supporting a row of books, these paragraphs hold the article together.

However, if you can't decide what would make a good opening, leave the introduction until later and start writing the main body of the article (see Chapter 15 for more on this). Once the majority of the article has been written it will be easier to focus on the right way to start your piece. Even if you have decided on your opening paragraph it may need altering once the article is completed.

When you are writing the first draft of an article, concentrate on expressing the ideas clearly and coherently as explained in Chapter 11. Try to write the first draft in the style that is appropriate for the chosen magazine, but focus on content to start with.

Opening paragraphs

If your opening doesn't grab the editor's attention, they probably won't buy your piece, reasoning that their readers won't bother to read it. Many magazine readers tend to browse, glancing at titles and openings before deciding whether to stop and read the article.

Your opening sentence needs to be short, snappy and interesting in some way – intriguing, arresting or shocking. Keep the rest of the paragraph short too, so that the reader can absorb it in a glance – many house styles only use one sentence in the first paragraph. A long opening paragraph gives the impression that a stodgy article will follow.

Insight
Typically opening paragraphs are half the length of the average paragraph for the rest of the article.

The opening sets the tone for the rest of the article, establishes the writer's viewpoint and, most importantly, contains the hook that draws the reader in.

If your subject is complicated, difficult or obscure, you will need to find an approach to the opening that grabs the reader's interest without misleading them about the nature of the article. More often than not, the solution to this problem is to find a human interest angle to the opening.

There are fairly strict rules about opening paragraphs in news stories. Magazine writers are allowed more freedom than news journalists but it is worth noting some of the more important news rules for openings, and using them unless there is a good reason not to:

▶ **Use nothing that needs explaining:** *jargon, foreign words, unusual abbreviations and complicated statistics.*
▶ **Use nothing to slow the reader down:** *complicated sentences with subordinate clauses, long difficult words, items in parentheses (e.g. brackets).*
▶ **Use nothing that creates typographical problems:** *figures, italics.*
▶ **Use nothing that needs quotation marks.**

Types of opening paragraph

An opening paragraph can be constructed in various ways. The different types can also be combined. Types of opening include:

▶ *a provocative, intriguing or surprising opening statement*
▶ *an anecdote or narrative*
▶ *a scene-setting or atmospheric description*
▶ *a question that grabs the reader's attention*
▶ *information (facts or figures) that is unusual enough to be striking*
▶ *analogy*
▶ *symbol*
▶ *humour*
▶ *irony*
▶ *personal remark*
▶ *quotation.*

A PROVOCATIVE, INTRIGUING OR SURPRISING OPENING STATEMENT

This is the most common opening and works well for all types of article. Aim for colour and contrast in the sentences that follow. For example:

> *Forget Alton Towers. For the ultimate white-knuckle ride you can't beat a trip with the crack RAF parachute team, the Falcons.*

AN ANECDOTE OR NARRATIVE

This adds human interest to stories that may be a little abstract, and is also a good way to start a celebrity feature or interview:

> *Greg Smith worked for the same company for 35 years and paid thousands into his pension fund. Six months before he was due to retire, the company became bankrupt and Greg's pension pot disappeared into a financial black hole.*

A SCENE-SETTING OR ATMOSPHERIC DESCRIPTION

The writing needs to be more novelistic than journalistic, but don't go on for too long:

> *Barking dogs, filthy black mud, festering pools of faeces-strewn water, and a pile of rags that turns out to be a sleeping human being. Not a scene from Dickens, but London in the twenty-first century.*

A QUESTION THAT GRABS THE READER'S ATTENTION

This should be used with care, since if it isn't pitched right it will irritate rather than intrigue:

> *How big is your carbon footprint?*

INFORMATION (FACTS OR FIGURES) THAT IS UNUSUAL ENOUGH TO BE STRIKING.

One in five exhausted housewives are saying 'No sex please, we're too tired' according to a recent survey.

ANALOGY

An analogy uses a comparison as a way of explaining something – it starts with the familiar, and uses that to help the reader understand the unfamiliar:

Have you ever tried to pat your head and rub your stomach at the same time? Flying a helicopter is like that, only harder according to Air Sea Rescue pilot Eddy Herbert.

SYMBOL

Select an item from your material that sums up, or symbolizes, the whole thrust of your piece:

When the owners of Manor House couldn't afford to fix the roof, they applied for a grant for £5,000. They were turned down. Now, 20 years later, it will cost £5 million to restore the derelict building.

HUMOUR

Useful in light-hearted pieces but don't use it inappropriately:

I love children – but I couldn't eat a whole one.

IRONY

Irony works by meaning the opposite of what the words appear to say:

Why should I worry about my carbon footprint? It's not as if I actually need this planet to live on.

PERSONAL REMARK

Start with your own experience of the topic you are about to discuss. Your experience needs to be relevant and interesting:

> *I've been homeless. I slept rough for a week after I was evicted from my student flat and was too ashamed to tell my parents. But that is nothing compared with Gary's experience. He has slept under the railway arches every night for six years.*

Beware of turning the introduction into an ego-trip; your readers won't be interested unless you are very well known to them.

QUOTATION

This isn't allowed in newspapers, partly because it isn't always instantly understood, partly because the convention is not to use quotation marks at the very beginning of a news piece, and partly because it makes awkward reading. However, it can be effective for some magazine articles, particularly if the person being quoted is either a household name or at least someone who has a good reason to be heard:

> *'Abuse is the theft of the magic of childhood,' says Valerie Howarth, executive director of ChildLine. How many children are still being robbed, and what can we do about it?*

Work in progress

We could open our stop smoking article in many ways, but the personal remark works well. Readers won't feel they're being talked down to by a non-smoker if it starts with the writer's own experience:

> *I found it very easy to start smoking, but almost impossible to give up. After several abortive attempts I finally managed it after a health scare a year ago. So what did I do wrong, and why is it so hard to stop?*

Closing paragraphs

Market research shows that some readers not only glance at the title and opening of an article before deciding whether to read on, they also skip to the last paragraph before deciding. And quite possibly the editor will do the same before deciding whether to buy your piece. The questions in their minds are something like: 'Is it really going to be worth all the bother of reading this? Am I going to get to something worthwhile out of it?'

Your ending needs to interest those people, and it also needs to provide a satisfying resolution for those people who have read the entire article. It must appear to follow quite naturally from the main part of the article. Never 'tack on' an ending.

Insight

If you are struggling to find a good ending, think back to the intention behind the article. The ending should show that you have achieved what you set out to do.

It's human nature to prefer an ending that is upbeat, so try to find something in your notes that will enable you to end on a positive note. If what you have to say is entirely gloomy then write a downbeat ending, but you will find it hard to place the article.

Different types of ending include:

▶ *summary*
▶ *surprise*

- *advice*
- *quotation*
- *statement*
- *anecdote*
- *description*
- *looking forwards.*

SUMMARY

This is the simplest type of ending and probably the most common. If the research has led to a conclusion then summarize it to make a strong straightforward ending:

> *I still don't think I would want to make a parachute jump, even though the Falcons made it look so easy. But should I have another chance to go up with them I wouldn't mind being harnessed up to look over the edge of the ramp. Possibly.*

SURPRISE

If your research throws up something unexpected, save that for the ending:

> *And as for that piece of London waste ground, it is now a community garden. After extensive decontamination it is a fertile flower-filled oasis in the middle of the city.*

ADVICE

Articles that explore other people's problems can slip into voyeurism unless the writer focuses on the wider implications. The ending is a good place to do this:

> *If your entire pension is a final salary scheme that is only with one company then it may be time for you to explore how you would manage without it. Look at your savings, investments and any property you own as well as making*

sure that your National Insurance contributions are up to date. Don't bury your head in the sand and end up like Greg.

QUOTATION

This is an effective way to end articles based on more than one interview. Save something good for the end:

Eddy loves his job in Air Sea Rescue, as he says, 'It's the combination of skill and danger. My wife complains that I can rescue someone from a cliff in a howling gale but I can't work the washing machine.'

STATEMENT

Look for contrast or drama. End with a bang not a whimper:

Reducing your carbon footprint might mean giving up a few things. But that has to be better than giving up the planet.

ANECDOTE

This is a good way to end a profile – save something interesting about the subject to end with:

Gary says he's ready to stop being a statistic. He has been allocated a flat and is nerving himself up to move into it. With help from the people at the shelter he has spruced himself up. He looks so good now that homeless people ask him for change.

DESCRIPTION

An article that is heavy on fact and light on human interest can be lifted at the end with a descriptive passage or anecdote:

But while the survey showed that women are taking on more and more roles normally associated with men, such as putting up shelves and servicing the mower, not all of them wanted men to help with the dusting – as one of them said, 'He'd only get in the way.'

LOOKING FORWARDS

If you can't find anything positive to end with in the current situation, try looking into the future:

Today, surrounded by scaffold, Manor House looks like an old lady with a zimmer frame, but with the funding secured and work about to start, there are high hopes for the future of this lovely old building.

Things to avoid

There are a few things to avoid in endings:

▶ **speech or essay-type ending:** *these commonly return to the introduction as a way of rounding things off. In an article the final paragraph can echo the opening paragraph but must arrive at a new position.*
▶ **questions:** *it is possible to end with a question that challenges the reader, but it is very difficult to do without causing irritation or confusion, so is best avoided.*
▶ **anything uncertain:** *the ending needs to be bold and confidently expressed.*

Work in progress

The stop smoking article will have included human interest, through the interviews, and factual information about ways to stop smoking. It could end in various ways, but a positive note with an advice element is the most helpful to readers:

The single most important element in giving up smoking is your motivation. Once you decide to do it, then you will do it. Do it now. You know you can. After all, I managed it and I was a 100-a-day smoker so it was really difficult for me.

Exercises
▶ *Write the opening paragraph of your article.*
▶ *Write the closing paragraph of your article.*

10 THINGS TO REMEMBER

1   *All articles need a beginning, middle and end.*

2   *Opening and closing paragraphs hold the article together.*

3   *It's OK to write the introduction after the rest of the article.*

4   *Keep the opening paragraph short.*

5   *Opening paragraphs must grab the reader's attention.*

6   *The whole article leads up to the closing paragraph.*

7   *Upbeat endings are more satisfying to readers.*

8   *An ending can echo the opening but must arrive at a new position.*

9   *Avoid ending with a question.*

10 *Avoid uncertainty in an ending.*

15

The main body

In this chapter you will learn:
- *to link the opening to the main body*
- *how to use quotations*
- *about transitions.*

> *What single piece of advice would I give to an aspiring feature writer? Keep the reader in mind: keep thinking 'How will what I'm writing capture someone's imagination?'*
>
> Helen Tovey, Editor, *Family Tree Magazine*

After the opening paragraph has set the tone, the rest of the article should flow smoothly, with one paragraph following logically on from the previous one. This is achieved by using bridging paragraphs at the start of the article to move from the opening into the main body, and by transitions (sometimes known as links) within the body of the article.

Bridging paragraphs

These come immediately after the opening paragraph and as the name suggests they connect it with the main body of the article.

In a simple feature, or one that is very accessible to the reader, there is no need for a bridge and the opening paragraph will lead quite naturally into the rest of the article:

> Opening paragraph: *Greg Smith worked for the same company for 35 years and paid thousands into his pension fund. Six months before he was due to retire, the company became bankrupt and Greg's pension pot disappeared into a financial black hole.*
>
> Second paragraph: *For years a final-salary pension scheme was thought to be the most desirable but recent events have turned that thinking on its head.*

However, if the subject of the article is one that readers may not immediately connect with, then you will need a bridging paragraph. Like the opening paragraph it must show the reader that the article will be relevant and interesting, but it also has to give an indication of what the article is about. There are three basic types:

- *nub*
- *background information*
- *context.*

THE NUB PARAGRAPH

The function of the nub paragraph is to tell the reader exactly what the article is going to be about. For example:

> Opening paragraph: *I've been homeless. I slept rough for a week after I was evicted from my student flat and was too ashamed to tell my parents. But that is nothing compared with Gary's experience. He has slept under the railway arches every night for six years.*
>
> First sentence of nub paragraph: *Gary became a statistic after a particularly violent row with his stepfather.*

This shows that the main content of the article is about how many people are homeless.

BACKGROUND INFORMATION PARAGRAPH

This shows what the main area of the article is about, but does not specify the particular thrust.

Opening paragraph: *'Abuse is the theft of the magic of childhood,' says Valerie Howarth, executive director of ChildLine. How many children are still being robbed, and what can we do about it?*

Background paragraph: *Nationally, at least 1,000 children a day speak to ChildLine counsellors, half of them suffering from physical or sexual abuse. Several thousand more are unable to get through. This does not mean the incidence of child abuse is rising but increasing publicity means more people are becoming aware of it.*

This gives the reader some more background information about the scale of the problem. However, this paragraph needs to be followed by a nub paragraph in order to complete the beginning of the article.

Nub paragraph: *Talking about it, however, is not sufficient; positive action is needed from the public in reporting suspected cases.*

The reader now knows that the article will be about asking the public to become aware of child abuse and to do something about it.

CONTEXT PARAGRAPH

This tells the reader the circumstances surrounding the main thrust of the article.

Opening paragraph: *Forget Alton Towers. For the ultimate white-knuckle ride you can't beat a trip with the crack RAF parachute team, the Falcons.*

Context paragraph: *Despite my dislike of flying, a chance to watch this prestigious team in action was not one to be turned down. So, a quick trip to the airport where we were met by the Falcon's leader, Lt Steve Darling, and there was the Hercules, with the inside of its cavernous fuselage looking pretty basic.*

The context paragraph now has to be followed by a nub paragraph to tell the reader what the article will be about.

Nub paragraph: *Personally, I couldn't think why anyone would want to jump out of a plane over and over again – but here was my chance to find out.*

The reader now knows that the main thrust of the article is going to be about sky divers and why they enjoy jumping out of planes.

Work in progress

Opening paragraph: *I found it very easy to start smoking, but almost impossible to give up. After several abortive attempts I finally managed it after a health scare a year ago. So what did I do wrong, and why is it so hard to stop?*

Background paragraph: *I have read in several articles and also seen on various websites I've looked at that nicotine is highly addictive and it only takes a few puffs to get us hooked. In fact, according to some experts it is the most addictive substance known to man. And once we are hooked we fall prey to the hundreds of dangerous chemicals found in tobacco smoke, including hexanal, formaldehyde (used for embalming) benzene, ammonia (used in dry cleaning) arsenic (used in rat poison) carbon monoxide (found in exhaust fumes) and methanol (used in rocket fuel).*

> **Context paragraph:** *Overcoming an addiction, as I discovered, is one of the hardest things to do. It takes tremendous willpower and motivation. But is that sufficient or is it necessary to seek help in the form of nicotine patches or hypnotherapy?*
>
> **Nub paragraph:** *Earlier this year I followed the efforts of five women and one man for six months as they battled to stop smoking.*

Main body copy

There are several types of content in the main body of all magazine articles:

- ▶ *information*
- ▶ *background/history*
- ▶ *opposing viewpoints*
- ▶ *quotations and anecdotes*
- ▶ *analysis, assessment, opinion.*

Most articles will have more than one element.

INFORMATION

Every article will involve some hard facts, and some articles will be nothing but – for example, a 'how-to' article. If the brief is for a 'how-to' article, then there is no point in trying to be clever with the writing. There is a big enough challenge in trying to convey precisely, and in the correct order, how the reader should set about the task under consideration.

Other factual articles do need some thought. Readers won't plough through articles that are little more than lists of facts and figures. Try to use fact boxes for some of the information, such as:

- ▶ *basic information that most readers will know but some may not*
- ▶ *information that is subsidiary to the main thrust of the article*
- ▶ *information that is more easily presented in a box, such as statistics.*

Insight

Charts and diagrams are useful for information that lends itself to visual presentation. These might be better written separately to go in fact boxes rather than cluttering up the main article.

Having moved some of the information out into the extras, you should be left with the hard core that needs to be in the main body copy. Work out the order that you want to present the facts in and try to write simple sentences that allow the reader to absorb them one at a time.

> *The facts: The Falcons give 120 displays a year. Free fall lasts 50 seconds. The plane must be in right spot before the jump. They practise in California.*

If at all possible break up the facts and figures with descriptive or anecdotal passages

Example

With a maximum of 50 seconds free fall the team needs plenty of practice all the year round to get the various formations right. Winter practice takes place in California.

Once the right altitude had been reached the cargo doors were opened and a few brave souls were harnessed up to look out over the edge of the ramp. When the plane was in exactly the right spot, accurately worked out according to height, wind speed and even the team's reaction time to the command 'Go', the smoke canisters were lit and the team ran down the ramp and away.

> *The team gives 120 displays a year and can do several*
> *different jumps over a weekend. After the display in Weston*
> *they were going on to Carlisle.*

However, if this is not appropriate for your brief, or for the
magazine, then take a disciplined, controlled approach. This is
particularly important in business-to-business journalism. Readers
of trade press are often under time pressure, and they need to
access the relevant information quickly and with minimum effort.

Work in progress

Adding comment to a statistic:

*Surveys show that 70 per cent of smokers want to give up
and there are many reasons why they should. Their life
expectancy will go up, they will look better, feel better and
even their sex life will improve.*

Insight

Figures should always be correct, but in trade magazines they
need to be absolutely precise, whereas in consumer magazines
they can be rounded up or down to whole numbers, which
are easier to absorb.

BACKGROUND/HISTORY

This sets the scene for the article but may not form a large part,
probably one or two paragraphs:

> *There are still a few final salary pension schemes, but they are*
> *fast disappearing as companies find them too difficult to fund.*
> *Because the retiree is guaranteed a pension based on their*
> *final salary, these schemes need to have large funds available.*

OPPOSING VIEWPOINTS

If the article is about a contentious subject, the writer will have to decide whether to nail their colours to the mast and slant the article in one direction or whether to present both points of view equally and fairly. See Chapter 19 for an example of presenting both points of view.

QUOTATIONS AND ANECDOTES

Anecdotes should bring some aspect of the article to life and engage with the human interest of the subject. They are often used in first person articles or in interviews which are written in the first person.

Clearly interviews and profiles will be constructed mainly out of anecdote and quotation, coupled with some background information. The number of quotations used will depend on the type of article, but most will benefit from at least one. They fall into two categories:

▶ *those spoken by an interviewee*
▶ *those which have been written, e.g. taken from a book, magazine or document.*

Insight

With articles which include a variety of information such as statistics, background research, direct quotes and opposing viewpoints, there may be more than one order of writing the main body. Just move paragraphs around until you find the best sequence.

Work in progress

Anecdotes from the interviews help to lighten the tone of our stop smoking article.

> *After her failure with the nicotine patches, Roberta found it hard to get motivated again – until her husband gave her a jam jar. 'He told me to put my cigarette money in the jar every day and he said when the jar was full I could spend it on whatever I wanted. We were broke at the time and the idea of being able to treat myself was irresistible. Every time I wanted a cigarette I just thought of my jam jar.'*

Spoken quotations

During the course of an interview the writer will have made notes. A decision will have to be made as to how the content of those notes will be used in the article. Either by:

- *direct quotes or reported speech, in quotation marks*
- *indirect speech preceded by 'that'.*

Use direct quotes from the interviewee if they are:

- *short, succinct or pithy*
- *contentious*
- *emotional*
- *close to the heart of the interviewee*
- *explain a situation clearly.*

Example
Sgt Tony Isherwood explained that being selected for the Falcons was the equivalent of playing football for England. 'It's the top of the ladder,' he said, 'and there is a lot of competition to get in.'

Note that there are strict conventions about how to attribute quotes in a news story but magazine writers have much more freedom. In news, the first time somebody is mentioned the attribution is best placed at the beginning, before the quote, although there is the option to put it after the speaker's first full sentence.

It goes without saying that direct quotes should be accurate, and if the writer has any doubts about what the interviewee actually said then they should check back with them. It is asking for trouble to attribute direct quotes to someone which are inaccurate. That is not to say that the odd grammatical error cannot be corrected (see below). When it comes to swear words and obscenities, each magazine will have its own rules about how to represent them. As we have already seen, speech is often rambling and ungrammatical and it is not necessary to reproduce this exactly.

Example

Gary actually said to the journalist:

'It's about respect, innit, bleeding respect, know what I mean, people don't, I mean to say, I never get none, I just get a load of abuse and stuff. Tossers.'

This was reported as:

'It's about respect, innit, I never get none, I just get abuse.

Note that for the quote the writer cleans up most of Gary's grammar and shortens what he says without losing his vocabulary ('respect', 'innit', 'abuse'). In doing that, some of the colour of his speech is lost, and the writer has to decide in each case whether it is important to try to restore that in the shortened quote. Try to let the speaker's voice come through – this is where taping interviews really comes into its own, although good shorthand is nearly as helpful.

Quotes should also accurately reflect the stance of the interviewee – don't cherry-pick quotes to suit your article at the expense of the interviewee. This may sometimes work in the pressurized world of the national press, but if you want a magazine to use you again, it is important to have a reputation for honest and accurate reporting.

Other material from the interviewee can be compressed into indirect speech. However, when doing this, it is important not to alter what the interviewee meant:

He admitted that he had been nervous about his first free fall jump but now his only apprehension was giving the spectators a good show.

Written quotations

These will have turned up in the course of your research and need to be very short and correctly attributed:

Some people believe that writing ability is innate, but others think it can be developed. As Lesley Bown and Ann Gawthorpe say in their book, Write a Play And Get it Performed: *'Can anyone be a successful writer? That will depend partly on talent, partly on luck but mostly on hard work.'*

You can also summarize the quote in your own words, but again you should give the attribution:

Some people believe that writing ability is innate, but others think it can be developed. Certainly Lesley Bown and Ann Gawthorpe (in their book, Write a Play And Get it Performed) *see writing success as being mostly hard work with a sprinkling of talent and luck.*

ANALYSIS, ASSESSMENT AND OPINION

Many articles inevitably carry an element of assessment, analysis and opinion:

Then came the white-knuckle bit. To complete the display the Hercules has its own routine to go through, including a sharp descent from 12,000 to 200 feet to fly low over the parachutists as they land. I know now what a 2.5g force feels like – it flattens your face and makes it difficult to breath.

There is an important distinction to be made between the writer's own opinions and those of interviewees and organizations. Always make it clear to your readers whether you are expressing your own views or explaining the views of others:

> *'They ought to be strung up,'* he added, *'hanging's too good for them.' While this may seem harsh, we have to remember what Mr Smith has suffered.*

This clearly shows that this is the opinion of the interviewee.

A think piece that is based on personal opinion still needs well-reasoned argument to be convincing. The emotional element should be balanced with hard information.

One area where the reader expects the journalist to have an opinion is in reviewing – see Chapter 21 for more on this.

Work in progress

Adding an interviewee's opinion:

So how well does hypnotherapy work? Julie, who smokes 60 cigarettes a day, is desperate to give up. She has tried the therapy several times and has become completely disillusioned. 'It had no effect on me at all,' she said. 'It is a complete waste of time and money, it's just a con.'

Transitions

Transitions are achieved by using linking words. These can link clauses within a sentence, sentences within a paragraph and paragraphs within an article. While it is perfectly possible to write paragraphs in isolation from one another, it makes for more comfortable reading if linking words are used to connect them.

However, a judgement will have to be made as to whether the linking words aid the flow of the article or whether they have become empty words (see Chapter 13). For more information on linking words, log on to the grammar websites listed in Appendix B.

Work in progress

So how well does hypnotherapy work? Julie, who smokes 60 cigarettes a day, is desperate to give up. She has tried the therapy several times and has become completely disillusioned. 'It had no effect on me at all,' she said. 'It is a complete waste of time and money, it's just a con.'

However, this has not been the experience of Jason, who used to be a chain-smoker. He said, 'Everyone ought to do it. I mean I just went along to see the bloke in my lunch hour and now look at me. I used to be coughing and hacking first thing, couldn't wait to have a drag. Oh yes, I'd recommend it, definitely. I mean it works, doesn't it? I used to have my first cigarette at 6.30 in the morning before

(Contd)

I'd even got up and now I have a cup of tea instead. I say to everyone give it a go, I mean it certainly worked for me, right?'

'However' at the start of the second paragraph leads the reader from a negative attitude to a positive one.

Exercises
▶ *Write the bridging paragraphs of your article.*
▶ *Write the main body copy of your article.*

10 THINGS TO REMEMBER

1 *Write to capture the readers' imagination.*

2 *Paragraphs should follow a logical order.*

3 *Using bridging paragraphs to link the opening with the rest of the article.*

4 *Use fact boxes if the article has a lot of statistics.*

5 *Check all figures, statistics and numbers for accuracy.*

6 *Use charts and diagrams if these make it easier for the reader.*

7 *Break up paragraphs of information with descriptions.*

8 *Use direct as well as reported speech.*

9 *Make sure any quotes used are true and accurate.*

10 *Present both sides of an argument fairly.*

16

Second drafts

In this chapter you will learn:
- *to improve the style of your article*
- *about the technical terms of style*
- *about vocabulary*
- *how to conform to guidelines.*

> *New writers' work almost always lacks structure and direction. They try to make up for this by taking the reader on a personal ramble through their thoughts, but this is NOT the same as injecting personality into a well-structured piece.*
>
> Tim Rumball, Editor, *Amateur Gardening* magazine

Two drafts should be enough for a magazine article, although while you are learning the necessary writing skills you may need more. Think of the second draft as the final polish, and discipline yourself to work to a tight schedule.

Rudyard Kipling, who was a journalist before he was a poet and novelist, coined the rule of six questions – Who, What, Why, Where, When and How? – to ensure that he covered every aspect of a story. Strictly speaking these relate more to news stories, but it is always a good idea to check that, where relevant, these questions have been answered in your article.

As you read, you'll notice things that could be improved – make a note and keep reading to the end. Now is the time to decide what the article needs – is it nearly there, or is it a complete disaster?

Insight

If there's enough time, don't look at the article for a few days after you finish the first draft. Do something else – research for another article, or some magazine analysis. When you go back to the article you will be refreshed, and you'll be able to read it with a clear mind.

Style

If your first draft was about content, the second should be about style. It is easy to be dismissive of style as mere window dressing, but finding the right way to express something can make a huge difference to how the reader understands the content.

The style needs to be appropriate to the subject matter, the magazine and the readers. Go back to your magazine research and refresh your feeling for their preferred style. Style enhances content, but don't use it to embellish.

Look

The article should be interesting to look at physically as well as being interesting to read. It is off-putting to see a page of uniform blocks of type. Where possible, have a mixture of direct and indirect speech. Vary the length of sentences and paragraphs. Judicious use of dashes and brackets adds a bit of colour. However, these must not conflict with house style.

One aspect of the look of an article is the crossheadings. Most magazines will insert those at the sub-editing stage, but a few leave it to the writer to put them in. Check with the editor about this.

Adding verbal colour

Many of us enter journalism because we were good at English at school, without realizing that the dry approach of our science teachers is probably more appropriate. The sample guidelines in Appendix A are trying to force us to let go of all the clever little tricks that worked in school essays, Christmas round robins and club newsletters, and to focus on getting the facts across. They are all about writing as plainly, clearly and simply as possible, and this is what you should have done in your first draft.

However, the well-known writers who have constructed the guidelines over the years have been a little disingenuous. Read some of George Orwell's journalism and you will find that it is full of colour and life. Moreover, the 'New Journalism' that came out of America in the 1960s and 1970s – with practitioners such as Hunter S Thompson, Tom Wolfe and Truman Capote – isn't plain at all. Their pieces have a strong novelistic and creative element.

The answer to this is that the guidelines are trying to tell you that content is king. So although content must take precedence over style, now is the time to decide what will bring your piece to life and make people want to read on. Very plain writing can feel stiff and unnatural:

> *Greg explained that his employers lost all of the pension fund during a recession. He is now entirely reliant on the State Pension and finds that he cannot manage, especially now that his wife is ill.*

This is very plain, and could be rewritten to convey more of the despair that Greg feels:

> *Greg's employers lost all of the pension fund during a recession. His eyes fill with tears as he tells me that he struggles to manage on the State Pension alone. He wants to buy little luxuries for his wife, who is recovering from breast cancer surgery.*

Don't, however, overdo it:

> *Greg's employers lost all of the pension fund during a recession. After 40 years' loyal service, Greg is reduced to the State Pension and he feels insulted. It's horrible to watch a grown man sob like a baby. His wife is desperately ill, and yet he can't afford the things she needs.*

Not only do you actually lose some of the power of Greg's suffering by over-describing it, but you alienate those readers who manage on the State Pension without complaining.

Using a colourful vocabulary can also help bring someone to life:

> *Despite living on the street, Gary is a bit of a dude. His head is shaved, his nose is pierced and his tatts are beautifully done.*

Technical terms

Many of us use these ways of playing with language without knowing the correct name for them. This brief list runs through some of the commonest ways of adding colour to your writing. All of them should be used with restraint:

- ▶ **alliteration:** *using the same initial letter, as in 'world wide web'.*
- ▶ **antithesis:** *contrasting two opposing points, as in 'Ask not what your country can do for you – ask what you can do for your country'.*
- ▶ **assonance:** *the musical effect of similar sounding words, as in 'Listen, listen, can you hear the hiss of the grasses?'*
- ▶ **hyperbole:** *exaggeration, as in 'Elvis was the greatest singer that ever lived'.*
- ▶ **litotes:** *the opposite of hyperbole, i.e. understatement, as in 'Elvis wasn't half bad'.*
- ▶ **metaphor:** *using an image to describe something, as in 'Last night Elvis gave us his full-throttle version of the song'.*

- ▶ **onomatopoeia:** *words whose sound echoes their meaning, such as 'buzz' or 'quack'.*
- ▶ **oxymoron:** *combining opposites, such as 'bitter-sweet'.*
- ▶ **simile:** *a type of metaphor that uses 'like' or 'as', as in 'She's as cold as ice'.*
- ▶ **syllepsis:** *incongruity, as in 'He fell down the stairs and in love at one and the same moment'.*
- ▶ **non sequitur:** *Latin for 'it does not follow', a word or statement which bears no relationship to the one before it in the same sentence, as in 'Buxom with blonde hair, Jessica's use of the split infinitive caused her to fail her exam'. The fact that Jessica failed her exam has nothing to do with the way she looks, so the two statements should not be lumped together in the same sentence. This is a common error made by writers when they are trying to cram too much information into a short piece.*

Vocabulary

There is always more than one way to say something, and in English there are usually a lot of choices – so much so that we have a separate book (or piece of software) called a thesaurus that gives all the synonyms*.

Inevitably a writer will have to decide whether to use the same word many times in an article or whether to use synonyms. Using the same word will give a strong element of repetition, which can create an unwanted effect of emphasis. Using lots of synonyms can be unsettling for the reader, or create the impression that the writer is showing off.

Consider an article about 'The meaning of happiness in the twenty-first century'. The thesaurus gives the following synonyms for happy: content, pleased, glad, joyful, cheerful, blissful, exultant, ecstatic, delighted, cheery, jovial. That's 11 possibilities, without

*synonym: word that means the same as another word

even thinking about idiomatic phrases such as 'in high spirits' and 'over the moon'. The answer is to use a simple word ('happy') and repeat it throughout the article as a basic term. Because it is a simple word it won't grate on the reader's ear. Then at key points, for emphasis or to get the reader's attention, use a synonym or idiom.

Fine-tuning

READ OUT LOUD

Once you have got a good first draft – that is, one where the content is clearly and logically expressed, it's time to look at the fine-tuning. Start by reading the article out loud, or better still, ask someone to read it while you listen. This has the effect of taking the article outside of your head and into the world, and will throw any flaws into relief. Make notes as you listen, but don't interrupt.

You will soon notice if any sentences are too long or clumsily put together. Repetition will stand out (but bear in mind that repetition can be useful for emphasis or important points). You will also get an idea of the rhythm of your writing and whether there is enough variety in it.

Do a rewrite based on your notes as soon as possible, while it is all still fresh in your mind.

MURDER YOUR BABIES

This common writer's phrase means simply 'take out anything that you are especially pleased with'. The chances are you were just showing off so discard them and rewrite in a more straightforward way. Of course, there will be times when you write something you are proud of and it should stay in. If you are undecided, leave the decision for a day or so and come back to it with fresh eyes.

TOO MUCH INFORMATION

After doing hours of research and interviewing, it is tempting to use everything you have discovered or noted down, but this can overload the article with too many facts, figures, and too much background information. Be realistic and only use what is necessary – you need to strike a balance between providing sufficient information and making the article so jam-packed that it becomes unreadable.

> **Insight**
> Even though you have amassed plenty of information, rather then trying to cram everything in use the extra material in another article.

Conforming to guidelines

LENGTH

Count the words in your piece as you write it. Computer software will do this for you, otherwise keep rough counts as you go along.

If your article is too long, you will have to shorten it. There are three ways of doing this:

- ▶ *cut*
- ▶ *summarize*
- ▶ *divide*.

CUT

If you simply have too much material, consider cutting something out. If your brief was to look at ways of amusing children in a holiday resort, then you can take out one or more of the less impressive options. An article based around a series of interviews can have one or more interviews removed.

SUMMARIZE

Older readers were probably taught at school to précis a piece of work – that is, to reduce its length without losing any of the meaning. These days it is often called 'summarizing'. If you feel that all the content of your article is essential and there is simply nothing you can cut, then you will have to summarize it.

Decide how many words you need to lose in order to fit the brief then check for:

- ▶ *unnecessary words and phrases*
- ▶ *adjectives, adverbs and qualifying phrases*
- ▶ *repetition*
- ▶ *descriptions*
- ▶ *yourself.*

Unnecessary words
You should always be on the lookout for these but now is the time to double-check. Phrases like 'put more simply it can be said that' and 'however, all things being equal' are not necessary. Take them out, you don't need them.

Adjectives, adverbs and qualifying phrases
Check every single qualifier that you have used and ask yourself if it is essential. Does your reader really need to know that Gary is 'tall, skinny and red-haired', or that Greg walks 'quickly, like a man who is late for an appointment?' If these add essential colour, then keep them – otherwise take them out.

Repetition
Repetition can be a stylistic trick for emphasis, or a way of keeping the piece focused on an important point, but if at all possible you should take it out.

Descriptions
You may have put some description in to give texture to a piece on a dry subject, but it almost certainly isn't essential. Take it out, and see how the piece reads without it.

Yourself
Little anecdotes and remarks about yourself can be a sort of writer's nervous tic. Again, take them out and see how the piece reads without them.

Key sentence
If you still have too many words, check each paragraph for its key sentence then rewrite the paragraph using fewer words – but make sure you keep the sense of the key sentence.

DIVIDE

If your article is still too long, consider whether it can be divided to make two separate articles. This might be a better option than producing a piece that is so elliptical and densely packed that it is almost unreadable.

If you have established a good relationship with the editor, say that you don't think the topic can be handled in the number of words specified and ask if you can have more space.

REWRITING

As well as shortening an article, rewriting can lengthen one that is too short and improve one that you are not happy with. Start by reducing it to an outline. Go through it paragraph by paragraph and create a series of headings, one for each paragraph. Now check through the headings and see if they make sense. Compare them with your original writing plan – did you stick to it or did you let yourself become distracted?

This exercise is likely to show you if there is any weakness in the structure of your piece. It may be just a case of moving paragraphs around to create a better flow, which is easy enough on a computer. If you are working with hard copy, try cutting the pages up into individual paragraphs and playing around with them.

If you decide that you need a complete rewrite, then go back to the planning stage (Chapter 11) and start again.

Insight

Be prepared to be ruthless when writing the second draft. You only want to send out your best efforts so now is the time to make sure it conforms to the magazine's requirements in length, style and content.

Work in progress

Looking through our piece on smoking we made the following changes.

Background paragraph:
I have read in several articles and also seen on various websites I've looked at that nicotine is highly addictive and it only takes a few puffs to get us hooked. In fact, according to some experts it is the most addictive substance known to man. And once we are hooked we fall prey to the hundreds of dangerous chemicals found in tobacco smoke, including hexanal, formaldehyde (used for embalming) benzene, ammonia (used in dry cleaning) arsenic (used in rat poison) carbon monoxide (found in exhaust fumes) and methanol (used in rocket fuel).

This paragraph is much too long, does not keep focused on the points which need to be made and has too many chemicals listed in it. We rewrote the first sentence which cut the number of words and clarified the focus. Then we chose three chemicals to use as examples, picking those

(Contd)

which were most interesting and which the readers would relate to.

It is generally agreed that nicotine is highly addictive and it only takes a few puffs to get us hooked. In fact, according to some experts it is the most addictive substance known to man. And once we are hooked we fall prey to the hundreds of dangerous chemicals found in tobacco smoke, including formaldehyde used for embalming, arsenic used in rat poison, and methanol used in rocket fuel.

An alternative would have been to move the list of chemicals to a fact box.

Main body:
However, this has not been the experience of Jason, who used to be a chain smoker. He said, 'Everyone ought to do it. I mean, I just went along to see the bloke in my lunch hour and now look at me. I used to be coughing and hacking first thing, couldn't wait to have a drag and then I'd chain smoke all day. Oh yes, I'd recommend it, definitely. I mean it works, doesn't it? I used to have my first cigarette at 6.30 in the morning before I'd even got up and now I have a cup of tea instead. I say to everyone give it a go, I mean it certainly worked for me, right?'

Again this paragraph is too long, so we took some of Jason's speeches and combined them into one short indirect speech about recommending the therapy. We kept his best quotes for direct speech, but slightly changed the order so that the paragraph ended with an interesting point – he now has a cup of tea instead of a cigarette.

However, this has not been the experience of Jason, who used to be a chain-smoker. He said that he'd recommend everyone to give it a go. 'It certainly worked for me. I used to have my first cigarette at 6.30 in the morning before I'd even got up and now I have a cup of tea instead.'

Final paragraph:

The single most important element in giving up smoking is your motivation. Once you decide to do it, then you will do it. Do it now. You know you can. After all, I managed it and I was a 100-a-day smoker so it was really difficult for me.

The last paragraph is often the one which remains in the reader's mind. In this article it should leave them encouraged. At the moment the writer is having an ego trip and probably all the reader will remember is the writer's problems. We cut the last sentence to give the paragraph impact.

The single most important element in giving up smoking is your motivation. Once you decide to do it, then you will do it. Do it now. You know you can.

Exercises
- ▶ *Write a second draft of your article concentrating on the style.*
- ▶ *Read the article out loud, or ask someone to read it to you.*
- ▶ *Murder any babies and check if there is too much information.*
- ▶ *Check that your article conforms to the guidelines of your target magazine.*

10 THINGS TO REMEMBER

1 *Take a break before writing your second draft.*

2 *Focus on the requirements of your target magazine.*

3 *Vary the length of sentences and paragraphs to add variety.*

4 *Use a few dashes and brackets to add colour.*

5 *Add verbal colour to avoid stiffness in writing.*

6 *Use synonyms to avoid over use-of certain words.*

7 *Avoid clichés.*

8 *Murder your babies.*

9 *Remove unnecessary words.*

10 *Read your article aloud to check it flows.*

17

Presentation

In this chapter you will learn:
- *about the importance of presentation*
- *to check your facts*
- *about layout.*

> *Read the magazine you're pitching to! I can't believe how many people still send me suggestions for 'an article about how to get fit' or 'a regular travel column', when we run nothing of the sort in Radio Times and are not likely to either.*
>
> Gill Hudson, former Editor, *Radio Times*

Once you have written the article, you need to make sure that it is professionally presented. If you send in anything that's scruffy, hasn't been spellchecked or is badly laid out then you probably won't be commissioned by that editor again.

When the editor is satisfied with the article, it is passed to the sub. Their job is to rewrite if necessary, cut if necessary, ask you for more material if necessary, write headlines (or accept yours) and write any crossheadings if required.

Insight

Don't rely on the overworked sub to improve your article, always send the best work that you can do. This means spellchecking your article, rechecking that all facts and figures are correct and getting names spelt correctly and job titles written out accurately.

In America the big publications employ fact-checkers who check, double-check and sometimes even triple-check the facts in an article. However, in the UK the responsibility for fact-checking falls on the sub, who is also expected to understand the law and to raise any legal issues relating to your article. Of course, the sub may well ask you to double-check your facts rather than do it themselves.

You should check all of your facts yourself before submitting the article. If necessary, provide a list of contacts and sources for the sub to conduct their own checks.

Finally, after the article has been typeset, the sub or another staff member will check the proofs*. Because of time constraints you are unlikely to see the proofs, and occasionally articles appear with mistakes or alterations that were not the writer's responsibility. If seeing the proofs is very important to you, all you can do is offer to visit the magazine's office and check the proofs on site. Your offer may well be turned down though.

Because of this, it is vital that you keep a copy of the article as you submitted it, together with all the notes you made during your research. With hard copy*, take a photocopy and keep it somewhere safe. With electronic copy, make a back-up* and keep it safe, and in a different room from the computer. See Chapter 26 for more on making back-ups.

***proofs:** roughly printed pages that are checked for spelling, layout, facts and so on before the final version is printed

***hard copy:** anything printed or written on paper

***back-up:** a copy of work on a computer which can be accessed if the original is lost. Back-ups can be both on another part of the computer's hard disk or, more usefully, on a separate piece of hardware or on the internet.

Hard copy and electronic submission

Eventually hard copy will be phased out, but at the time of writing we are in transition. Many magazines still accept hard copy and some still prefer it, especially from writers they haven't used before. Once your article is accepted, the editor may well ask you if you are able to send an electronic copy on disk, CD-ROM or by email. If you can't, it means that somebody in the magazine office will have to type your article into the computer system.

Layout – hard copy

There are well-established conventions for laying out hard copy that still apply (but check each magazine's guidelines too).

First create a cover page with the following information:

- ▶ *title*
- ▶ *your name*
- ▶ *word count*
- ▶ *number of pages*
- ▶ *number of photos, if any*
- ▶ *your contact details.*

Then lay out your article as follows on good quality, A4 white paper:

- ▶ *wide margins all round on all folios* – top, bottom and sides*
- ▶ *double-line space the text*
- ▶ *two double-line spaces between paragraphs*
- ▶ *indent first line of each paragraph*
- ▶ *number the folios and show how many pages there are altogether – for example 'page 1 of 8'*

*folio: page

- ▶ *no paragraphs to run across from one folio to the next*
- ▶ *catchline* on each folio, preferably at the top*
- ▶ *'more' or 'mf' (meaning 'more follows'), at the bottom right of each folio except the last*
- ▶ *'ends' on last folio at end of article*
- ▶ *after 'ends' your contact details and the word count.*

Don't staple the folios together, if necessary use a paper clip. If there are photos or illustrations, create a separate sheet with the captions for them. Head the sheet with the catchline. Number each caption and number the photos or illustrations. Never write directly on the back of a photo, use a sticky label.

Write a brief covering letter with the following information:

- ▶ *title of article*
- ▶ *your name*
- ▶ *short reference to your brief*
- ▶ *which rights you are selling (see Chapters 6 and 8)*
- ▶ *request for copy of the issue containing the article.*

Finally, check with the editor whether an invoice is required.

Layout – electronic copy

There is currently no industry standard approach for electronic copy and you will have to check with each publication what they would prefer. If you are emailing, ask if they accept attachments – at one time many large organizations wouldn't accept attachments in case they contained viruses. Things are also complicated by the fact that most publishers use Mac computers and software, whereas many amateur journalists use Microsoft Windows.

*catchline: unique word or phrase to identify an article

As a default, use the following:

- *a first page with the same information as for hard copy*
- *Times New Roman, 12 point*
- *double-line spacing*
- *indent each new paragraph*
- *number the pages as for hard copy*
- *a footer with a catchline to identify the article*
- *'ends' at the end of the article*
- *your name, contact details and the word count after 'ends'*
- *a list of photo/illustration captions.*

Email the covering letter and invoice as separate attachments, and be sure to mention the catchline on both the letter and the invoice.

Insight

Before you post your article make sure you have either another hard copy on file or a back-up copy on your computer, preferably stored in a different place to your computer.

Exercise

- *Organize the presentation of your final draft.*

10 THINGS TO REMEMBER

1 *Ensure you are sending the article to the right kind of magazine.*

2 *Check to see if the magazine wants hard copy or accepts emailed articles.*

3 *If there are no guidelines, use double-line spacing as a default.*

4 *Layout the article according to the magazine's guidelines.*

5 *Check spelling and grammar.*

6 *Number the pages.*

7 *Put the article title at the bottom of each page in case they get separated.*

8 *Put your name at the bottom of each page in case they get separated.*

9 *Create a cover page with your details, the title of the article and its length.*

10 *Take a copy either paper or electronically and keep it safe.*

18

Illustrations

In this chapter you will learn:
- *about different types of illustration*
- *about sources for illustrations*
- *some basics for taking your own photographs.*

> *What can new writers do to help get their articles accepted?*
> *Good pictures! Almost all mainstream gardening magazines*
> *depend heavily on good photography, so before you embark*
> *on an article, think how it can be illustrated/photographed*
> *(and what it might cost).*
>
> Tim Rumball, Editor, *Amateur Gardening* magazine

There is no doubt that smaller publications are far more likely to take your article if you can also provide illustrations – in fact some specify this.

'Illustration' in the magazine context has two meanings:

1. *A blanket term meaning all pictorial matter, for example, in a proposal letter 'I can provide illustrations in the form of photographs'.*
2. *A more specific term meaning non-photographic pictorial material, for example, in a proposal letter 'I can provide both photographs of myself and an illustration taken from my book, drawn by the artist A. Gawthorpe'.*

Most articles require illustration of some sort, and there are various sources for these:

▶ *library illustrations organized by the magazine or the writer*
▶ *copyright illustrations organized by the magazine or the writer*
▶ *originals created by the magazine*
▶ *originals created by the writer*
▶ *freelance photographer.*

LIBRARY ILLUSTRATIONS ORGANIZED BY THE MAGAZINE OR THE WRITER

There are many picture libraries and agencies listed in the *Writers' and Artists' Yearbook* as well as on the internet (see Appendix B). For a fee they will provide photographs to illustrate any topic.

If you use websites which offer free photos, check the terms and conditions to ensure you can use them in a published article. Also check that the free photo does not have any copyrighted designs or logos in it. If it does, either don't use it or get permission from the holder of the copyright.

If you know of a suitable photograph which has appeared in another magazine or newspaper it is always worthwhile contacting them and asking if you can use it in your article.

COPYRIGHT ILLUSTRATIONS ORGANIZED BY THE MAGAZINE OR THE WRITER

If your article requires a specific illustration, such as a famous painting, you will need to track down the owner and obtain their permission. However, this can prove to be very expensive if the painting or object belongs to a museum or art gallery.

ORIGINALS CREATED BY THE MAGAZINE

Larger publications will have their own art department and will be able to produce illustrations or organize photographs. Smaller publications won't have this facility, and will be dependent on picture libraries and writers themselves.

ORIGINALS CREATED BY THE WRITER

If you have a lot of talent, or are a trained graphic artist, you can provide drawings to illustrate your articles. However, most writers concentrate on providing photographs.

FREELANCE PHOTOGRAPHER

If you don't have the facilities or the expertise to take your own pictures, or live too far away from the area or object you want photographed, use a freelance photographer. Find one either by calling the local papers in the area or contacting the British Institute of Professional Photographers or Royal Photographic Society.

Insight

Be aware of copyright rules. This means you can't use someone else's photograph without their permission. However, some photographs may be in the public domain and can be used by anyone. Always check because it could be expensive if you are taken to court.

Photographs

At the top end of the trade, photography is a highly skilled creative art and very few of us have the talent and dedication to master it. However, many magazine articles are illustrated with photos taken by the journalist with only basic skills and equipment.

Insight

Look at your target magazine and assess the photographs before deciding whether to attempt taking your own. If they look as if they have been taken by a specialist photographer,

(Contd)

it might be better to use a professional photographer or buy pictures from an agency.

CAMERAS

Unless you plan to take a lot of photographs to illustrate your articles, it is probably not worthwhile spending a lot of money on a new camera. If you do decide to buy a new one it is better to go for an SLR-type digital camera with at least 8 mega pixels because they have bigger imaging sensors and you can get filters for them (see below).

FILM AND DIGITAL

If you are using a conventional camera, the film must be a minimum of 35 mm, as this allows for enlargement. Use lower film speeds to give finer grain and better detail.

With digital cameras use the largest file size your camera will shoot with. These take up more room in the memory but will give higher quality prints. Magazines like bigger files as they give quality and flexibility. Aim for a 5″ × 7″ image size and 8 to 9 megabytes file size. Don't confuse the number of pixels with file size – fewer pixels and a larger file size sometimes gives a better quality.

Basic principles

Here are some basics that beginners need to take on board:

- ▶ *Get images sharp by focusing accurately and using the right shutter speed.*
- ▶ *Take plenty of photos so you have choice. One in ten will probably be usable.*
- ▶ *Take portrait as well as landscape orientations.*
- ▶ *When using a digital camera, turn off the facility that puts a date on every photo.*

- *Try to use natural light wherever possible.*
- *Use a tripod or steady the camera by resting it on a suitable surface. Miniature tripods are useful pieces of equipment – they can be carried in a pocket and used anywhere.*

It is important to have contrast between the subject and the background. You can achieve this by:

- *getting the sky behind the subject (try squatting down)*
- *using contrast lighting*
- *using a larger aperture* and faster shutter speed* on the camera to bring the subject into focus (or setting an automatic camera appropriately).*

COMPOSITION

Think about the composition of the photo before you take the shot. Modern digital cameras have the great advantage of allowing you to see the picture as soon as you've taken it, but the small screen size means you don't always appreciate problems with the composition and detail.

Putting the subject right in the centre of a picture can make for a very uninteresting composition. Instead, imagine the picture divided into thirds (like a noughts and crosses grid) and place the subject on one of the intersections.

Photos don't always have to be taken at eye level – sometimes standing on a chair to get an elevated view of a group of people will create a much better picture. If the activity is going on at ground level then crouch down to take the photo.

---

*aperture: the opening in front of the camera lens that lets the light in when the picture is taken and which is measured in 'f-stops'. A larger aperture has a lower 'f-number'. If you are reasonably close to the subject then a large aperture will make the subject the main focus of the picture.

*shutter speed: the amount of time the shutter opens to allow the photograph to be taken

Finally, make sure that there are no unfortunate juxtapositions such as poles or notices sticking out of the tops of people's heads.

CROPPING PICTURES

If you are using a digital camera this is a useful facility because any mistakes made when composing the picture can often be rectified by cropping. This can be done in the camera or on the computer. However, check with the magazine that they will accept cropped pictures because some prefer to crop the pictures themselves to suit the page layout.

FILTERS

With conventional cameras you can use filters to improve the quality of the picture. However, they do demand a degree of expertise. Here is a list of the basic ones:

- **polarizing filters:** *create the azure blue skies and sparkling scenery found on postcards. They also improve water shots by cutting down reflections.*
- **ultraviolet filters:** *cut down on haze and protect the camera.*
- **neutral density filters:** *reduce light levels and are used to lengthen exposure times, useful when photographing water to create a feeling of movement.*
- **graduated filters:** *used to darken skies which are bright against a darker foreground to balance the overall exposure in a picture, or to add colour to skies.*

TAKING THE BEST DIGITAL PHOTOS

It is possible to use filters on SLR-type digital cameras which have a lens with a thread, but compact digital cameras don't have a thread so any improvements to the photo will need to be done by changing the settings on the camera. All digital cameras have a white balance setting and it is worthwhile checking to see what other facilities your camera has, such as sharpening colours, increasing or decreasing the contrast, and sharpening the image.

WHITE BALANCE

The colour of light reflected off an object will change according to the colour of the light source. A white object will reflect a different colour in sunlight to artificial light. Our eyes adjust to this automatically and we always see the object as white, but cameras have to be programmed to do this and this process is called the white balance adjustment.

The camera's default white balance is set up to give good results under most circumstances, but to get the best picture it might be necessary to adjust it according to the prevailing conditions such as sunlight, fluorescent light, cloud, shade or flashlight.

MANIPULATING FILE IMAGE

Nearly all digital images which have been taken without a filter will need some adjustment on the computer to get the colour and contrast right. However, sharpening on the computer can cause printing problems in the later stages of the production and should be left to the printer.

RETOUCHING PHOTOS

Depending on what software you have it is possible to remove red eye and get rid of unsightly objects such as electricity pylons. Again, check with the editor whether the publication will accept retouched photos.

Types of picture

There are several types of pictures used for illustrating articles:

▶ *people*
▶ *animals*
▶ *buildings*

▶ landscapes
▶ action.

PEOPLE

Most people photograph better if they are taken three-quarter face rather than full face. This can be achieved by having them stand a quarter sideways and then turn their head towards the camera. Also use this technique when photographing presentations between two people, but make sure they stand very close together. It may look and feel unnatural, but it will make a better photograph. Although it is not essential to have the subject looking directly at the camera, don't have them looking out of the picture either.

When taking groups of people, again make sure they all stand very close together so that there are no gaps between them and if possible, have them interacting with each other. Unless it is essential for the article don't have any background showing. Also, unless it is essential for the article, do not take very large groups or crowds of people as they do not make good photographs.

People on their own often dislike being photographed, so giving them something to do or to hold relaxes them and makes them look more natural. It can help if you position them, then ask them to look down at the ground. On your request they should look up and smile. If you snap them at that moment you will capture a much more natural expression than the usual frozen smile.

Some pictures are enhanced if the person is framed in some way, such as looking through an arch or surrounded by flowers. If necessary get them to sign a model release form giving you permission to use the photos.

PHOTOGRAPHING CHILDREN

This can be a minefield because of legislation to protect them. Ensure you have written permission from the parents to take the photos and get them to sign a model release form so that you can use them.

Basically, this is a form signed by a photographic model which agrees that the photographs taken of them belong to the photographer, and gives the photographer the right to use the photographs in the ways specified. However, they can be adapted for use by members of the public.

It is easy to design your own release form and there are plenty of formats to be found on different websites which could be followed (but bear their copyrights in mind). What you need to include are:

▶ *your name and address as the photographer*
▶ *the name and address of the subject of the photograph*
▶ *wording to show that the subject grants the photographer full copyright of the photographs and agreement that the photographer can use them, wholly or in part, in any magazine or newspaper*
▶ *place for the subject to sign with the date*
▶ *provision for a parent or guardian to sign if the subject is under 18 years old.*

A good photo will catch the child's personality and the secret is to be patient until the child relaxes and starts to cooperate and then be quick before the child gets bored.

Insight

It is preferable not to name the children in the caption, but if you do, only use their first name.

Take photos from different angles, not forgetting to get down on hands and knees to the child's level if necessary. It is particularly important to take a lot of shots so that you have choices. And don't forget to turn on the red eye removal facility to stop them looking like little devils.

ANIMALS

Photographing animals can range from taking a prize-winning mouse to a herd of bison. Many of the principles are exactly the same as those for photographing children – be patient, be quick, catch their personality and take plenty of shots.

Large animals such as horses are best taken sideways on or three-quarters sideways. Take care not to get them out of proportion – if they turn their head towards you they can look as if they are all head. When photographing small animals, get down as close as possible to their level or put them on a suitable stand.

BUILDINGS

Modern buildings often look more striking if taken from an unusual angle. If taking older or traditional buildings, look for the most interesting aspect. If the most interesting aspect of a building is its size, include a person to give a sense of scale.

LANDSCAPES

This includes both country and urban areas. In open urban views try to get movement and animation by catching people going about their business or sitting and chatting. Also look for interesting side streets, unusual buildings and small squares.

Country views often look best early in the morning or towards evening when long shadows add interest. Misty conditions also add an extra dimension. Make sure the horizon is level and have the main point of interest slightly away from the centre. Some shots are improved by having someone in them. For example, a winding country lane looks better with a walker striding along it to give a sense of scale and movement.

ACTION

This includes people working as well as sports. Most digital cameras have the facilities for taking dynamic action shots. Be sure to take plenty so you can choose the best one.

Pictures

PRINTING PICTURES

If you are using film have your photos printed in 5" × 7" format (unless the magazine has other requirements). Even if you are using a digital camera, some magazines still want printed pictures so you will need to print them off. Unless your printer is a very good one this should be done professionally. Either take them on a CD-ROM to a shop or send them online to an internet company (see Appendix B).

CHOOSING PICTURES

With prints spread them all out. With digital pictures download them onto the computer so you can study them on screen. Look for pictures that tie in with what you say in the article and that are lively and interesting in their own right.

SENDING PICTURES

Hard copy will need to be posted in a reinforced envelope. Digital pictures can be emailed (submit as high quality jpegs at 300 pixels per inch) or downloaded onto a CD-ROM and posted. Ask the editor which they would prefer.

CAPTIONS

However you send your photos, they will need to be numbered and captioned. The captions should give full information about the photo answering the questions 'Who, What, Why, Where, When and How?' With printed photos, never write on the back of them, although you can stick a label on the back with your name and address and the photo's unique number. Some editors like the caption to be taped onto the back, while others prefer a separate sheet with the captions listed (and cross-referenced by the photo's number).

Digital photographs are given numbers by the camera. They can also be assigned names on the computer screen. Send the list of numbers or names with the relevant captions in a separate attachment.

Copyright

You own your photograph's copyright. If a magazine wants to use your pictures the best idea is to grant them a licence for a particular use, for example, to illustrate an article. If they want to use them for other purposes they will have to renegotiate with you and pay another fee.

The subject you are photographing may also be under copyright and permission to shoot is required in some areas. For example, you need permission to photograph in Trafalgar Square and Canary Wharf, and structures such as the London Eye are copyrighted as well as public sculptures. Also take care when photographing in sensitive areas. Taking pictures of or in railway stations, airports and even shopping malls can result in security descending on you. Best to play safe and either don't take photos there or get permission.

Exercises

▶ *Look at the article you wrote in Part one. How would you like to see it illustrated?*

▶ *If you have internet access, research one of the online picture libraries for suitable illustrations.*

▶ *Take some of your own photos to accompany the article. Only send them out with the article if you are convinced they are of professional standard.*

10 THINGS TO REMEMBER

1 *Buy a good camera to take your own photographs.*

2 *Learn how to take good photographs.*

3 *If using a digital camera, use the largest file size.*

4 *Take plenty of shots to give you a choice.*

5 *Use a tripod to keep the camera steady.*

6 *Try to get the subject doing something.*

7 *When photographing children and animals get down to their level.*

8 *Get the parents' permission before photographing children.*

9 *Photos taken in the early morning or evening sometimes give the best results.*

10 *If prints are required, send 5" × 7".*

19

Two articles analysed

In this chapter you will learn:
- *more about analysing an article*
- *more about research*
- *more about targeting an article to a particular magazine.*

What advice would I give a new writer? Don't overwrite.

Helen Tovey, Editor, *Family Tree Magazine*

We have already used parts of our own articles for some of the examples throughout the book, but in this chapter we have taken two complete ones for a full analysis. If you are interested in knowing more about Lesley and Ann, visit their website at www.freewebs.com/womenwhatwrite/.

Insight

One way of improving your writing skills is to analyse articles written by other people. Assess how the first paragraph pulls the reader in, how the next paragraph provides a good link to the main part of the article and how the writer concludes the piece.

Ann's article for *Horse + Pony*

(courtesy of *Horse + Pony*)

Analysed by Lesley: This article has been chosen for analysis because it is written in the third person. Although it was written several years ago, it also provides a good example of how to use information from interviews, using both direct and indirect speech, and how to handle two or more conflicting opinions.

PUBLICATION

The target publication was *Horse + Pony*, a fortnightly magazine aimed at horse riders.

AUTHOR'S EXPERTISE AND EXPERIENCE

Ann is a keen rider who has kept horses and who has entered dressage competitions. She started as a correspondent on her local paper, paid by the word, and was eventually taken on to the permanent staff. When she decided to branch out into magazines, *Horse + Pony* was an obvious choice because not only was she impressed with the quality and type of articles, but it came out fortnightly so needed more copy than the monthly magazines.

THE IDEA

The loss of the herd of wild ponies on the Quantocks was in the news at the time. The ponies were being taken off the hills because the National Trust had refused to put up a fence that would keep them off the busy main road.

THE ANGLE

Because Ann was aiming at a riding magazine, she angled the article to the welfare of the ponies. For other types of publication she could have angled it to, for example, how residents were likely to be affected, the role of the National Trust or the nature of the Quantocks landscape.

ASSESSMENT OF IDEA AND ANGLE

Wild ponies are of interest to the magazine's readers but are not covered very often. The readers are nationwide so Ann needed an angle on this local story that interested them, and the welfare and future of the ponies did that.

PROPOSAL

Ann originally sent the editor a list of article ideas and some of her clippings. For various reasons the editor didn't pick up on a single one of her ideas, but a follow-up phone call led to the Quantocks article being commissioned.

RESEARCH PLAN

Ann wanted to focus the article on Annabelle Walter's efforts to save the lives of the ponies, because she knew that the magazine's readers would be most interested in that aspect. However, she realized that in order for the article to be fair and balanced, she would have to interview the owners of the ponies, someone from the National Trust, and at least one representative of the local residents.

She also needed some background on the history of the Quantocks, the law relating to common land and the role of the National Trust.

ACTUAL RESEARCH

Because the article was written before internet access was common, Ann started her research by contacting the nearest Tourist Information Centre to the Quantocks. They were able to give her the phone number of the local library and from the library she obtained the name and phone number of the local newspaper, which had covered the story. A phone call to the reporter gave Ann some contact numbers and background information. A phone call to the National Trust headquarters gave her the name of the local Land Agent. The headquarters also sent some information on the National Trust. A visit to her own local library gave her some more background information.

Nowadays of course she would start her research on the internet for background details, cross-checking and contact names.
But the tried and trusted method of ringing around until you find the person, or the information, you want still works.

INTERVIEWS

Ann interviewed the following people, tracking them down by phoning around until she reached the relevant person:

- ▶ *Arthur Barrow – owner of ponies*
- ▶ *Mr Carslake – Land Agent for the National Trust*
- ▶ *Colonel Stokes – Quantocks warden*
- ▶ *Colonel Grandfield – Chair of Holford Parish Council*
- ▶ *Mr Franks – spokesman for the Quantocks Society*
- ▶ *Annabelle Walter – owner of an Animal Rescue Sanctuary*
- ▶ *Fred Stockham – owner of some of the ponies.*
- ▶ *The local journalist who reported the item originally.*

TITLE

'Plight of the Quantock Ponies' is an emotive title which also uses alliteration for effect.

PLAN AND ORGANIZATION

Ann found herself with a mass of material which she laid out as a series of headings. She quickly realized that what she had was a series of disagreements and that in each case she should put both sides of the argument. These are the arguments she untangled from her notes:

- ▶ *The ponies' owners wanted the fence, but the National Trust, local residents and the Quantocks Society didn't want it.*
- ▶ *The owners felt the ponies were at risk on the roads, but one interviewee quoted the local police as disagreeing with this. Ann was unable to track the source of this alleged police opinion, so had to be careful how she used it.*

- *Some people believed that the ponies were not hardy enough to spend the winter on the hills and that they should be housed for the winter rather than fenced onto the land, but the owners believed they were perfectly hardy.*
- *The owners said the ponies were never sold for meat, some people (who were not prepared to be named) felt that they were.*
- *The owners believed some of the ponies were too old to be re-homed but the owner of the sanctuary believed they could be re-homed.*
- *The National Trust believed the fence would be illegal but apparently wanted to keep the ponies to graze the land; local residents believed the fence would cause an increase in farming the common land; the Quantocks Society believed the fence would cause overgrazing by encouraging the keeping of sheep; whereas the owners believed the fence was the only answer to their problems over safety and the only way the ponies could stay on the hills.*

Ann also had some technical and historical information about the ponies, and a stack of information about the National Trust and the legal status of common land. In addition, a separate story concerned the money that was raised to pay for the fence, and another concerned the money that was needed to save the ponies by sending them to a sanctuary.

Ann organized the list of disagreements into an order that flowed, starting with the news item (the decision to take the ponies off the hills) and ending with the attempt to get them to an animal sanctuary. She could then see points where she could feed in some of the other information. Because her readers were primarily interested in horses, she set aside most of the information about the National Trust and the legal status of common land, (but knew she'd be able to use it in another article).

Her new list of points, placed in the order she wanted for the article, looked like this:

1 *Decision to take ponies off the land due to decision not to erect fence*

2 *History of ponies on the Quantocks and information about the ponies*

3 *History of the request for a fence*

4 *The money that was raised for the fence*

5 *National Trust's position*

6 *Other opposition to the fence*

7 *Concern over ponies' welfare*

8 *The ponies' future*

9 *Returning the money that was donated*

10 *The role of the animal sanctuary*

11 *The money needed to save the ponies.*

Item 1 is the natural place to start – this is a news background feature and has to start with the news item that has triggered it. However, knowing her readers, Ann quickly moves on to the kind of thing that horse-lovers are interested in, item 2. Items 3 to 6 bring the reader back to the main thrust of the article with some fairly dry material about the various disagreements. However, from item 7 onwards Ann can give her readers what they want with more information about the ponies, their welfare and their future. The stories of the money that was raised for the fence and the money that is needed by the sanctuary are interwoven within these items.

Ann considered adding extras in the form of fact boxes using the information she had about the National Trust and the status of common land, but decided that the article didn't need them.

OPENING AND CLOSING PARAGRAPHS

Ann's opening paragraph is deceptively simple:

> **In a blaze of media publicity and surrounded by circumstances which have split the local residents, the famous herd of Quantock ponies, in Somerset, is to be broken up.**

In fact it is cleverly constructed. In only 29 words it gives the nub of the piece. Note the most dramatic words, 'broken up', are saved for the end. In order to do this Ann had to use a passive construction. An active sentence would in this case have been far less powerful, for instance:

The Quantock Pony Breeders' Association has decided to break up the famous herd of Quantock ponies causing a blaze of media publicity and a split among local residents.

Ann didn't write her closing paragraph until she had finished the article. She originally intended to end with the discussion of the money needed to save the ponies, but she realized that this made rather a flat ending. She didn't want to take sides so she went for an anecdote:

Whatever the rights and wrongs of the situation the fact remains that the Quantock herd will soon no longer exist. A situation mourned by Fred Stockham, who in all his 73 years cannot remember a time when the ponies were not there. He commented, 'When the ponies come down off the hills, that will be it, for ever and a day!'

LINKING PARAGRAPHS AND MAIN BODY COPY

Ann's finished article has no need of paragraphs linking the opening with the main body copy. After the first two paragraphs about the news story she jumps to a paragraph of historical background. Because of the thought that went into the planning and organization the article has its own coherence.

ILLUSTRATIONS

Ann was not able to take photographs herself, but she contacted a local newspaper which had covered the story and they agreed for a small payment to supply a photo.

THE FINISHED ARTICLE AS SUBMITTED WITH COMMENTS

Plight of the Quantock Ponies

In a blaze of media publicity and surrounded by circumstances which have split the local residents, the famous herd of Quantock ponies, in Somerset, is to be broken up.

Short opening paragraph starting with the news item that readers may already have seen.

Following a decision by the National Trust not to allow a fence to be erected on its land, which would have prevented the ponies from straying, the Chairman of the Quantock Pony Breeders' Association, Mr Arthur Barrow said, 'We can no longer allow our ponies to be killed and injured on the roads.'

Another short paragraph continuing the news story and ending with more drama with the words '...killed and injured'. There is no link to the next paragraph.

The history of the ponies goes back over 100 years when the original herd of Exmoor ponies was turned out on 5,000 acres of common land. After the war the owners, who hold commoners' rights, decided to improve the quality and height of the ponies to make them more attractive for both children's and adults' mounts. They used Arab and part-bred Arab stallions to do this, the most famous of which was Waterfall who, Mr Barrow said, was the Champion Pony of Britain two years running.

The reader's interest should be engaged by now and so Ann can write a longer paragraph of historical information. Note though that it ends with an interesting titbit for the reader. Ann should have been more specific about 'the war' – although older readers know she means the Second World War, younger ones may not.

The ponies now grow up to 14.2 to 14.3 hh and are predominantly bays and chestnuts.

A very short paragraph about the ponies with the sort of specialist information of interest to her readers – she is answering the questions they would ask.

> *One, which was exported to Denmark, won every showing and jumping class in which it was entered and the owner still keeps in touch with the Breeders' Association.*

This sentence could have been included with the one above to make a single paragraph. It contains another interesting titbit for Ann's readers. There is a good link to the next paragraph as it ends with '…Breeders' Association' and the next paragraph is about the founding of the Breeders' Association.

> *It was in 1957 that Mr Barrow's father, Kenneth, and two other breeders, Jack Waterman and Fred Stockham, started the Association and although the ponies are not a registered breed themselves they are eligible for registration as part-bred Arabs.*

More historical and specialist information is fed in.

> *In September, every year, the herd is rounded up and driven down from the hills for the foals to be sold. In previous years, when there were up to 90 breeding mares on the hill, the sight of the wild ponies being herded down to the market attracted sightseers from far and wide.*

Ann is moving the article back to the present and the mention of the sales links to the next paragraph about the decline in the market.

> *The recent decline in the market for children's ponies, however, caused the breeders to cut back the size of the herd. Mr Barrow explained, 'We breed ponies for riding not for meat, and we only produce sufficient foals that we can comfortably sell.'*

> *At the present time there are 30 mares and two stallions on the hills, last year's crop of foals having already been sold.*

> *Problems with the animals straying onto the roads began
> a few years ago and the Breeders' Association asked for
> permission to erect a fence on the National Trust land along
> the edge of the main A39 road between the villages of Nether
> Stowey and Holford. This busy road carries tourist traffic
> to the West Country, and last year four ponies were killed.*

This paragraph gets to the heart of the article and starts to explain
the dispute about the fence. Note that Ann breaks a rule here when
she says 'last year'. She should have specified which year, as she
had no way of knowing when the article would be published.

> *Following media coverage at that time members of the public
> donated £13,000 to the Association to build the fence and
> save the herd. Mr Barrow said, 'We were overwhelmed by the
> response, which ranged from a cheque for £5,000 to 50p from
> children's pocket money.'*

> *The Breeders' Association are particularly bitter that the
> public enquiry, which was to have been held to examine the
> matter, was called off after the National Trust said it would
> not be in the public interest for the fencing to be erected.*

This paragraph and the following six give a clear and balanced
account of the different factions in the dispute.

> *Mr Carslake, Land Agent for the National Trust, who own
> 800 acres of land in the area, explained, 'We are governed by
> the National Trust Act and we are restricted in what we can
> allow on common land belonging to us. Anything we do must
> be for the public's benefit.' He said that up until August of
> last year the National Trust had agreed to consider allowing
> the fence to be erected. However, so many people were against
> it that the Trust took Counsel's Opinion and were told that it
> would be illegal to allow the fence to go up.*

> *He added, 'The National Trust are not opposed to the ponies.
> On the contrary we would prefer to see them on the land as*

it is important to the future management of the hills to have them grazed.'

This point was also taken up by the Quantocks' Warden, Colonel Stokes, who said, 'If stock is removed, the hill will revert back to bramble and thorns.' He explained that he was in favour of the fence as much of his time was spent in chasing ponies off the road, and he pointed out that they are a tourist attraction.

Opposition to the fence comes from the local councils, the Quantock Society and local residents. They were at pains to point out that they were not opposed to the ponies, but feared that fencing the common land would be the thin end of the wedge and that gradually it would become farmed.

Chairman of Holford Parish Council, Colonel Grandfield, explained. 'A fence will allow an increase in the number of sheep on the hill and we were concerned that with intensive grazing the natural heathland would disappear.' He added that the police did not consider that the stretch of road was any more dangerous than similar stretches in other parts of the country.

The Quantock Society spokesman, Mr Franks, said, 'We have collected 2,000 signatures on a petition against the fence. People have a right to unhindered access to common land.' He thought the problem of accidents involving the ponies could be solved if the herd was taken off the hills in the winter. He added, 'We feel that the ponies are not hardy enough to be out all year round.'

By saving this point until last in her explanation of the different opinions, Ann is able to introduce the concept of worry for the ponies' welfare and link in to her next paragraph on that topic.

In fact, several horse lovers in the area expressed concern over the condition of the ponies and queried whether the animals are hardy enough to spend the winter on the hills. They feel that the tough constitution of the original Exmoor pony has been lost due to the breeding policy and that this is why they come down onto the roads, in search of food and shelter. They are also concerned that some of the foals have gone for meat, especially when the meat price is high.

Ann knows that her readers will hate the thought of the ponies going for meat. If she had made too much of it early on she may well have made it difficult for her readers to appreciate all sides of the discussion. Placed here it raises the emotional content of the piece and leads on to the climax of the article.

The Breeders' Association deny this and maintain that all the foals go to private homes. They also dispute the idea that the ponies do not winter out well and say that hay is put out in bad weather.

The climax is delayed for one last balancing paragraph.

Following last week's meeting of the Breeders' Association, when it was decided to disband the herd, Mr Barrow said, 'There are at least ten mares who are too old to go to new homes and these will be humanely destroyed.' He felt very strongly that is was kinder to put them down than force them to adapt to a new environment. He pointed out, 'These ponies are wild and used to running free over hundreds of acres, it would be cruel to confine them to a small acreage.' The ponies' future is now under discussion.

He was certain that suitable homes would be found for the rest and said, 'The ponies will go back to their owners who will decide how to dispose of them.' He added that this could take several weeks as the mares are in foal and cannot be rounded up. 'They will be collected as they come off the hill.'

As for the £13,000, which had been donated, he was hopeful that, after a meeting of the Quantock Commoners, this would be returned to the senders. He said, 'We have the names and addresses of 90% of the people, and I anticipate that the remaining money will be given to a horse charity, possibly Riding for the Disabled.'

Answering the question that readers are bound to ask – what will happen to the money?

Leading the campaign to save the ponies is Miss Annabelle Walter, BHSAI, who runs the Heaven's Gate Animal Rescue Sanctuary near Langport. She said, 'These ponies deserve a chance.' She is particularly concerned to save the older mares from slaughter despite the problems which can be expected with wild ponies.

Annabelle is brought in right near the end of the article, untainted by any of the disputes and appearing rather like the cavalry riding over the hill. A series of short paragraphs follows. By keeping them short Ann allows the point of each one to stand out clearly.

She pointed out, 'The Sanctuary specializes in rescuing foals so we are quite used to dealing with unhandled animals.'

She is looking for homes where the mares can be left to run free and where more than one pony can be kept. She added, 'I wouldn't try to home any pony if I wasn't certain that it would adapt to its new environment.'

Her aim is take 12 ponies at a time, worm and de-louse them and then place them in suitable homes, which have been checked. The ponies will only be lent to their new owners and can come back to the sanctuary at any time.

She said, 'The outlook is fairly good, already several of the breeders have provisionally agreed to sell their ponies to me.'

Naturally, all this is going to take a good deal of money and Annabelle said, 'I would like to suggest to the people who sent money to the Breeders' Association to save the ponies that when it is returned to them they re-donate it to me.'

This is a very subtle appeal for money – there is nothing to stop readers from making a donation.

> **Whatever the rights and wrongs of the situation the fact remains that the Quantock herd will soon no longer exist. A situation mourned by Fred Stockham, who in all his 73 years cannot remember a time when the ponies were not there. He commented, 'When the ponies come down off the hills, that will be it, for ever and a day!'**

And finally human interest and an anecdote to finish.

Insight

There are two sides to every story. Be sure to give equal weight to both. The reader will trust your conclusions more readily if they feel you've been fair and unbiased.

Lesley's article for *Motorcaravan Motorhome Monthly*

(courtesy of *Motorcaravan Motorhome Monthly*)

Analysed by Ann: This article has been chosen for analysis because it has been written in the first person and shows one way of writing reviews with a light touch.

PUBLICATION

The target publication was *Motorcaravan Motorhome Monthly* (*MMM*), a 370-page glossy magazine.

AUTHOR'S EXPERTISE AND EXPERIENCE

Lesley and her partner own a motorcaravan which they regularly use to travel around the country. Lesley had already sold a few articles to various magazines and was also a joke writer. She picked MMM as a magazine to target because they are regular subscribers to it and she knew that many of the articles were submitted by freelance writers.

THE IDEA

When the Caravan Club opened a new site at Hillhead in Devon it was a big change for them as it had a swimming pool, a bar, a restaurant and a shop. There was a lot of media interest in the opening but Lesley realized she hadn't read anything about what it was like to actually stay on the site. This gave her the idea for the article.

THE ANGLE

MMM runs regular reviews of different makes and models of motorcaravan which follow a set template covering all the aspects. Lesley's angle was to use the same template, but for reviewing a campsite.

THE HOOK

The first three paragraphs appear to suggest the article is a vehicle review, but they are ambiguous and the reader is intrigued.

ASSESSMENT OF IDEA AND ANGLE

Reviews of motorcaravan sites had not been featured in *MMM* in this way before so Lesley decided that giving a familiar idea a new angle would not only make an interesting article, but also one which would be useful to the readers.

PROPOSAL

Lesley contacted *MMM* and asked them if they would like a review of the new campsite. The editor was keen on the idea, and he didn't tie her to a tight brief because he already knew her work, but equally he didn't commit to taking the article until he had seen it. She agreed to go ahead on this basis.

RESEARCH PLAN AND ACTUAL RESEARCH

As this was a review the only way to research the project was to go and stay on the site and test all the facilities, which is what Lesley did.

INTERVIEWS

Because the template did not include interviews Lesley did not carry out any formal ones or use any quotes in the article. However, she did informally interview other site users and the staff for background information.

TITLE

The title 'Hillheaven or Hillhorror?' combines several title ideas: a play on words, alliteration and posing a provocative question. It also acts as a hook to draw readers into the article.

ORGANIZATION OF MATERIAL

Although Lesley assembled a mass of information about the site, the planning and organization of the information was comparatively simple because it had to follow an existing template.

OPENING AND CLOSING PARAGRAPHS

The opening paragraph:

> *It's always an exciting moment when a new model appears on the market. The media rush to scramble all over it, the public look at the brochure and compare the spec with their trusty old favourite and, inevitably, opinion is divided down the*

middle. Is it a new-fangled fad that won't last five minutes, or is it the shape of things to come?

This is a deliberately ambiguous to hook the reader.

The closing paragraph:

What can I say? Forget all your Hi-De-Hi nightmares, the new model is great. Hillhead is a lovely site with wonderful facilities. You can keep well away from them if you prefer a traditional Caravan Club experience, or you can indulge yourself with a little bit of motorcaravanning luxury. Either way, it's a winner.

This provides a satisfying end to a specialist review by combining a summary with an opinion and finishes with flourish – 'Either way, it's a winner.' As such it gives the readers exactly what they want from a review – a brief overview and a recommendation.

LINKING PARAGRAPHS

After the opening paragraph:

And when the new model has been produced by no less an institution than the Caravan Club, then you can practically hear the collective sharp intake of breath among the members.

The model in question is Hillhead, and once all the media furore had died down, Mike and I took the opportunity of a quiet little test drive of our own.

These two paragraphs continue the ambiguous description of what is to be reviewed right down to the last four words 'test drive of our own'. While non-*MMM* readers might still be thinking at this point the piece is going to be about reviewing a vehicle, regular *MMM* readers would already be suspecting it wasn't because they would know that Hillhead is not a vehicle – which is fine because this piece was aimed at regular readers.

MAIN BODY COPY

As discussed in Chapter 15, there are several types of content that can be found in magazine articles:

▶ *information*
▶ *background/history*
▶ *opposing viewpoints*
▶ *quotations and anecdotes*
▶ *analysis, assessment and opinion.*

Lesley's article uses just two: information and analysis, assessment and opinion. There is no background or history included because the remit of the article is to provide current information.

▶ *Information: the whole article is about providing information in a concise and logical format. It has to examine all aspects of the campsite and answer any questions that the readers might have in mind.*
▶ *Analysis, assessment and opinion: again, the whole article is about analysing, assessing and giving an opinion.*

Here the writer's honest opinion is balanced by agreeing that other people could well think differently. The paragraph also assesses the facilities.

> *One side of the courtyard is formed by the games room. I'll be honest, this left me cold – just some games machines and a couple of pool tables. But I suspect that if you've got children at that difficult tweenage stage – you know, 12 going on 19 – it would be a good place for them to hang out while you had a drink at the bar next door and kept a discreet eye on them. The courtyard is completed by the shop, toilets, and some of those mysterious doors marked 'Staff Only'.*

LINKS

Because it is a review, crossheadings, such as 'On the Road' and 'Wash and Brush Up', help to break up the article into logical sections and also conform to the template (the crossheadings in *MMM* are differently themed for each review but always follow the same order).

Within these sections, the paragraphs follow a logical progression and the use of link phrases such as 'Next to that', make for a smooth transition:

> *The media hype understandably focused very much on this area, and the children's play area with its amusing miniature motorcaravan (not a tugger's van you will note). We found there was quite a lot more to Hillhead than that. Behind the play area is a large field with a pair of football goals and what I think was probably a volleyball net.*

> *Next to that is another big field with a sectioned-off dog walk in one corner and a row of benches, strategically placed so you can enjoy the spectacular views of Torbay. In other words, vast amounts of space for ball games and general letting off of steam without annoying the neighbours.*

Phrases such as 'But also', show the reader that although the next two paragraphs are connected, they are going to be comparative.

> *So the presentation of this new model is pretty stylish, and its setting is beautiful – but is the standard maintained when you try living in it? At first glance, maybe not. It looks a bit, dare we say, scruffy. This is entirely due to the policy of letting some of the hedging and grass verges grow wild, and once your eye gets used to it, it's fine.*

> *But also, there are no hardstandings at Hillhead. We like it like that but it may not suit everybody. We visited after a week of rain and a few people were having problems with*

the mud and the slopes – however, the wardens were
more than happy to help with their little orange tractor,
and had put notices everywhere reminding you to ask
for help.

Because this is written in the first person the style of writing is personal, with the use of dashes for emphasis and made-up words such as 'tweenage' and 'blissier', to add colour.

ILLUSTRATIONS

Lesley took a lot of photos in and around the site and picked the best of them to send to *MMM*. They added one photo of their own where they weren't happy with hers.

THE FINISHED ARTICLE AS SUBMITTED WITH COMMENTS

MMM Live-In Test Report
Hillheaven or Hillhorror?
It's always an exciting moment when a new model appears on the market. The media rush to scramble all over it, the public look at the brochure and compare the spec with their trusty old favourite and, inevitably, opinion is divided down the middle. Is it a new-fangled fad that won't last five minutes, or is it the shape of things to come?

And when the new model has been produced by no less an institution than the Caravan Club, then you can practically hear the collective sharp intake of breath among the members.

The model in question is Hillhead, and once all the media furore had died down, Mike and I took the opportunity of a quiet little test drive of our own.

These three paragraphs are the hooks to draw the reader in and they set up the idea that this is going to be based on a typical MMM vehicle test article.

OUTSIDE

First, a look around the outside. Very smart. All new buildings, attractive shades of grey and soft green. New planting to the communal areas, which should mature nicely, and things left a bit wilder around the pitches, to encourage the wildlife.

We were particularly interested in the pool, or rather, pools. Side-by-side adults' and children's pools, outdoor, heated, with classy wooden loungers at the poolside. The adult pool has only one access point and could do with at least one more we thought.

At the end of the season hardly anyone was using the pools and opening hours were reduced, but the cheery lifeguard was there to keep an eye on us, and the water wasn't that cold. Our only problem was the day they closed early and we didn't realize – some sort of notice board would have helped.

The pools' facilities are completed by changing rooms/toilets, a cold drinks machine and two outdoor hot showers.

You approach the pools by walking through the courtyard, a sheltered area with tables and chairs and those alien-looking patio heaters. On a sunny day or a summer's evening this must be a lovely place to sit and relax.

One side of the courtyard is formed by the games room. I'll be honest, this left me cold – just some games machines and a couple of pool tables. But I suspect that if you've got children at that difficult tweenage stage – you know, 12 going on 19 – it would be a good place for them to hang out while you had a drink at the bar next door and kept a discreet eye on them. The courtyard is completed by the shop, toilets, and some of those mysterious doors marked 'Staff Only'.

The media hype understandably focused very much on this area, and the children's play area with its amusing miniature motorcaravan (not a tugger's van you will note). We found there was quite a lot more to Hillhead than that. Behind the play area is a large field with a pair of football goals and what I think was probably a volleyball net.

Next to that is another big field with a sectioned-off dog walk in one corner and a row of benches, strategically placed so you can enjoy the spectacular views of Torbay. In other words, vast amounts of space for ball games and general letting off of steam without annoying the neighbours.

These paragraphs follow the template and give a detailed analysis of the external facilities accompanied by a personal opinion. Lesley has tried to put herself in the readers' shoes and answer their questions.

ON THE ROAD

Hillhead is just outside Brixham in south Devon. There are a couple of route options for driving down there, all will be busy in the high season and OK for most of the rest of the year.

Although the site is so close to built-up Torbay it feels rural and peaceful. We didn't fancy the walk to the beach, which involves a risky stretch of road with no pavement, but a short drive brought us to a free National Trust car park and access to the coast path. We did two lovely circular walks on the path with wonderful views.

Another enjoyable trip involved crossing the River Dart on one of the two ferries from Kingswear to Dartmouth. Each trip only takes a few minutes but is great fun. Larger vehicles should take the Higher Ferry, which has a weight limit of 7.5 tons. Alternatively, catch a bus from right outside the campsite and travel as a pedestrian. Dartmouth is a pretty little town with interesting shops so well worth a visit.

Because this article is tied in to a template for a different kind of review, Lesley was forced to abandon a logical pattern of following a description of the outside facilities with a description of those on the inside. However, it does give plenty of information about where it is, how to get there and what you can do when you arrive. This is possibly the most strained part of Lesley's attempt to follow a vehicle review, since the 'On the Road' section would normally be about what it's like to drive the vehicle. She just about gets away with it.

INSIDE

So the presentation of this new model is pretty stylish, and its setting is beautiful – but is the standard maintained when you try living in it? At first glance, maybe not. It looks a bit, dare we say, scruffy. This is entirely due to the policy of letting some of the hedging and grass verges grow wild, and once your eye gets used to it, it's fine.

But also, there are no hardstandings at Hillhead. We like it like that but it may not suit everybody. We visited after a week of rain and a few people were having problems with the mud and the slopes – however, the wardens were more than happy to help with their little orange tractor, and had put notices everywhere reminding you to ask for help.

Hillhead is hilly and the site has been terraced into a series of small pitching areas. Many of these are divided by hedges into individual units, and I have to say some looked a bit on the small side for large outfits. However, there were other areas of more conventional layout with easier access. Overall the pitches felt secluded and many of them had views, a great combination.

WASH AND BRUSH UP

There are two huge and brand new amenity blocks, easily the best I've ever seen. They include a laundry room, family bathrooms (key at reception) and the most luxurious showers ever. The dressing area inside each shower cubicle felt larger than usual, and included a bench as well as hooks. However, somebody in their wisdom had chosen the flimsiest hooks imaginable, and they were already giving up the ghost after only a season's use. But the showers were basically gorgeous, and even the sink cubicles have a lockable door instead of a curtain.

Set against all this luxury the veg. prep and washing up area outside felt rather miserable and windswept – but the one we used was blessed with an outstanding view and anyway, washing up on holiday is men's work.

LOUNGING

Are you cursed with a sofa whose back is too low for comfort and a TV that only a contortionist can watch from the lounge area? Never mind. At Hillhead the bar is a warm comfortable room with a huge projection TV. I didn't ask how they decided which channel to watch, and in any case it's turned off when the entertainment starts.

There were three evenings of entertainment while we were there and we sampled one of them. Frankly, we didn't like it. I won't identify the culprit, but the second-rate singing and third-rate jokes didn't do anything for us. On the other hand, it was what my friends in the business call a cold audience. A few more drinks, a bit of dancing, and maybe it would have felt quite different, who knows?

KITCHEN

If we thought the washroom facilities were special, then the catering goes into a new dimension. Or rather, two dimensions. First there is the shop. We were there right at the end of the season, but the shop still had everything you could need. Opening hours were reduced during our stay, but that wasn't a problem. Such bliss to pop out for a pint or nip out for a newspaper. And even blissier to be able to send someone to buy his own breakfast.

And on those days when the thought of wielding the can opener makes you feel faint, there is the restaurant. Breakfast, morning coffee, lunch, dinner – whatever madam and sir desire. We had a mid-morning cup of tea sitting outside on the patio, and a dinner. Tea was the tea bag in a cup type of thing – perfectly acceptable, but I'd have liked a biscuit with it. The main kitchen closes mid-morning and hot drinks are made at the bar – a few biscuits or even cakes wouldn't be too difficult to arrange and would, after all, add to the takings.

Dinner was taken inside in the restaurant. This is part of the bar and entertainment room, which is L-shaped, with the food side being a No Smoking Zone (but no restrictions on eating with the smokers if you want to). There is a children's menu with all the usuals on it as well as a reasonably varied adult menu.

We are forced to test every restaurant we visit because Mike can't eat either wheat or dairy. First of all, the staff took great trouble to check the ingredients on their basic menu, and they weren't happy about any of the dishes. They were very keen to help, and made no secret of the fact that the dishes were bought in ready cooked and frozen. This late in the season there weren't many fresh cooked specials on the menu, but they were able to offer Mike a steak.

It was superb – a beautiful steak cooked exactly how he'd asked for it (sounds simple, but seems to defeat most chefs). He had chips and vegetables and they fried some onions just for him instead of the (battered) onion rings. I had a lasagne followed by a hot chocolate dessert and both were very tasty, of the pub food variety.

While we were eating the chef came out to check that Mike was happy. He said that next year there should be much more fresh cooked food available, so things will get even better.

SLEEPING

There is one thing about this new model that has been bothering some of us. Noise. Most of us like Caravan Club sites because they are so quiet. Have they shot themselves in the foot by trying to appeal to the rowdier element? No. My totally unscientific test reveals that the bar has been sited well away from the pitches and the noise just doesn't carry. We were at the far corner of the site and the nights were as starlit and peaceful as you could wish. Possibly those closest to the bar might be aware of it, but the answer is, choose your pitch with care.

CONCLUSION

What can I say? Forget all your Hi-De-Hi nightmares, the new model is great. Hillhead is a lovely site with wonderful facilities. You can keep well away from them if you prefer a traditional Caravan Club experience, or you can indulge yourself with a little bit of motorcaravanning luxury. Either way, it's a winner.

Extras: (these are part of *MMM*'s template)

SPECIFICATION

Caravan Club site

Non-members and tent campers welcome

207 pitches (plus 29 for tents)

This is Lesley's weakest section since in a vehicle review it would contain a lot of technical information. Lesley hasn't found anything similar to say about a campsite, although she could easily have included information about mobile phone and TV reception and the number of amps in the electric hook-up, all of which are of interest to motorcaravanners.

SUMMARY

We liked:

▷ *the pool*
▷ *the bar/restaurant*
▷ *the views*
▷ *the amenity blocks*
▷ *the lovely cheerful staff.*

We would have liked:

▷ *a biscuit with our cuppa*
▷ *a blackboard by the pool to show opening hours*
▷ *another access ladder into the pool.*

We disliked:

▷ *watching someone struggle to manoeuvre off their pitch (yes, we did go and help)*
▷ *the mud*
▷ *the entertainment.*

Insight

When analysing other articles take note of how the writer has used both direct and reported speech, has added verbal colour by clever use of descriptions and had made the piece look interesting on the page by varying the length of sentences and paragraphs.

10 THINGS TO REMEMBER

1 *Analyse several different types of article.*

2 *Badly written articles can be equally helpful if you can see where the writer went wrong.*

3 *News stories can be developed into a feature*

4 *Use a new angle on a standard format.*

5 *Small mistakes don't stop an editor from taking an article.*

6 *Choose magazines which offer the most opportunities.*

7 *Write about what you know.*

8 *Be prepared to come up with plenty of ideas.*

9 *Be prepared to do the necessary research if commissioned.*

10 *Be selective about what material to use – pick what is relevant for the readership.*

Part three

Specialist writing

20

Real life

In this chapter you will learn:
- *how to write interview-based articles*
- *to do research before the interview*
- *about profiles.*

Think in packages – an editor is more likely to take words and pictures that work together. If you get an exclusive interview, try to get exclusive photos to go with it.

Chris Jones, Editor, *Golf World*

Interview-based articles

Many articles are based around interviews, either of celebrities or non-famous people who have an interesting story to tell.

Celebrity interviews are almost always granted, if you have a commission from a magazine, because the person concerned wants publicity, for a book, a film or just for their career generally. They are usually arranged by publicists or agents, although someone at the start of their career may not have employed anyone as yet.

With celebrity interviews the journalist and the interviewee often have different agendas. This can be very extreme, such as when the journalist wants to hear all about an actor's marriage break-up but the actor wants to publicize their latest film. However, celebrities usually understand that in order to get publicity they may have to agree to talk about their private life. If they feel very strongly they will embargo certain topics before agreeing to the interview.

People who are not well known often enjoy their 15 minutes of fame for all sorts of reasons. These who have been through a trauma or tragedy may find the process of being interviewed therapeutic in a small way. Seeing their story in print can also help with the healing process. Of course, some people don't welcome media attention, so they are unlikely to grant you an interview.

Insight

When interviewing someone for a real-life article, ensure that all your questions have been answered. However, be prepared to be flexible and follow a new line of questioning if the interviewee reveals information you weren't aware of.

TRIUMPH OVER TRAGEDY

These type of stories are popular with many magazines and some publications feature nothing else. There is a market and some writers make a living out of ghost writing* these articles for other people.

CONDUCTING THE INTERVIEW

Celebrities are busy people and are likely to allocate a short length of time to an interview. Be well prepared, do your research beforehand and have a list of questions ready.

If you are interviewing someone who has had a difficult experience (such as a health problem) research the nature of the experience and familiarize yourself with any relevant technical terms.

*ghost writing: a writer produces work that goes out under another person's name

Insight

Build up trust with the interviewee by being professional but friendly. Don't allow the interview to become a chat and don't talk about yourself unless your experiences will help the interviewee to talk about theirs.

Email

Email is not a good way of conducting in-depth interviews that are going to form an entire article. However, some publications run formula series where the same questions are put to various celebrities, and they can be done by email. Some celebrities will have their publicity person compile the answers.

Phone

Telephone interviews are common in America where distances are greater and if you can develop good skills it is possible to interview people over the phone (see Chapter 10). If you are phoning someone with a traumatic experience to recount, be prepared to give them plenty of time. If they become upset, offer to hang up and phone back later.

Face to face

Celebrity interviews are usually conducted in hotel rooms with a publicity person present. This is not ideal, and you should aim for somewhere more personal if possible. You will be allocated a length of time and may find another journalist waiting outside the door when your time is up. In all of this the publicity person has a lot of power and keeping on their good side is essential.

Celebrities sometimes have the power to insist on copy approval but try to avoid agreeing to this. (Bear in mind, however, that celebrities are more likely to sue for libel than ordinary people.)

When dealing with non-famous people who have found themselves thrust into the limelight, the interview is likely to be taken more slowly as the interviewee will not be used to the process. They could well be very nervous, or suspicious of the press.

WRITING UP THE INTERVIEW

Once you start writing up the interview for your article, stay firmly focused on your brief and the publication it is destined for. For a celebrity interview you could imagine yourself being quizzed by a typical reader. Would they ask 'What's he like, is he sexy in real life?' or would they ask 'How does she get the ideas for her books?' You don't have to write the interview up in chronological order, but you mustn't change things in ways that distort the truth.

The same approach works for non-celebrity interviews – ask yourself what the reader will want to know. How did this woman lose 15 stone? How did she get so heavy in the first place? And so on.

Should you feature in the interview? This will depend very much on the style of the magazine and your status as a writer, but in any case do not turn the piece into an ego trip. Only bring yourself into the article if by doing so you help the reader to understand the interviewee better.

Example
A journalist finds that their tape recorder isn't working. The celebrity interviewee organizes new batteries. Recounting this shows the celebrity as both professional and kindly.

Profiles

This term is loosely used to describe articles that are written about someone from research rather than an interview. With celebrities, their agent or publicity person will often provide material, and earlier articles and interviews will be on record.

Exercise
▶ *Choose an incident or experience from your own life and write it up as an article.*

10 THINGS TO REMEMBER

1 Use your contacts to find interesting people to write about.

2 Do background research to add an extra dimension to the article.

3 Make a comprehensive list of questions.

4 Focus questions on what the readers will want to know.

5 Where possible, interview your subject face to face.

6 Don't be late or keep your subject waiting.

7 Don't prolong the interview, but keep to the time agreed.

8 Don't talk about yourself except in order to put the subject at their ease.

9 Write up your notes as soon as possible after the interview.

10 Check you have spelt the subject's name correctly.

21

Reviews and previews

In this chapter you will learn:
- *about the difference between reviews and previews*
- *about the qualities needed*
- *about the different types of review.*

> *Great reviewers are very disciplined writers. They have a strong voice, wide knowledge of the industry, and write with precision and authority, which gives their opinion validity. The reader needs to care about what the reviewer thinks.*
>
> Gill Hudson, former Editor, *Radio Times*

Most consumer magazines and newspaper supplements carry reviews of the arts and restaurants, as well as previews of the arts and also of products. Readers expect that the writer of a review will have personally experienced the subject of the review, whereas with previews readers understand that they are being given information on which to make their own judgement. For this reason, previews are often no more than rewritten press releases, although they can include elements of comment and assessment from the writer. A review should never be based on press releases or publicity material.

Previews are often written by staff journalists, but on a publication with a small staff, a freelancer may be commissioned to write a regular new product round-up or market news page. Reviews can be written by either staff or freelancers depending on the publication.

Breaking in

As with all journalism both reviewing and previewing can be difficult areas to break into. You may need to start by writing reviews without being paid – for one of the smaller magazines or a newsletter. Once you have some samples, put together a portfolio that you can send to editors. Be sure to mention any special or unusual areas of expertise that you have.

> **Insight**
> Make sure the knowledge of your field is up to date and keep it that way – you never know when you will get your chance. If you don't already have a good background in your chosen subject, make sure you become an expert before attempting reviews.

Qualities needed in reviewers and previewers

Reviews and previews should have the following qualities:

▶ *expertise*
▶ *the common touch*
▶ *passion*
▶ *open-mindedness*
▶ *opinion.*

EXPERTISE

You need to know enough about a subject to understand its frame of reference. Professional reviewers need to have broad knowledge of their subject. Occasional reviewers are usually commissioned on the basis of special knowledge, for example a book about butterflies would need a reviewer capable of assessing the content of the book. Of course, it would only be reviewed in the first place if the editor felt it was relevant to the magazine's readers.

THE COMMON TOUCH

It's easy, if one has expertise, to forget that most readers won't understand technical terms, abstruse references or complicated histories. Reviewers have to pitch their writing at a level that is appropriate for their readership.

PASSION

If you don't care about the subject, then you won't convey anything worthwhile to the reader.

OPEN-MINDEDNESS

A reviewer needs to bear in mind that readers may not share their personal likes and dislikes, and needs to be able to assess fairly evenly those things that are not to their personal taste.

OPINION

Where the public rely on a reviewer for an assessment of a product – whether that be a stage play or a restaurant – then the reviewer's personal opinion will come into play.

> **Example**
> Many of us use previews of television programmes when making our decision on what to watch. In most cases the previewer will have seen preview tapes of the programme and will be giving their personal opinion.

Aim of a review

A review is a critical assessment of its subject. This is not the same as an academic essay, because it aims to help the reader decide whether to invest time and money in experiencing the subject of the review for themselves. The only exception to this is television reviews, which are published after the programme has been shown (although of course a review of an episode of a series may well persuade the reader to watch the next episode).

The reviewer acts as a bridge between the reader and the item under review. The reviewer brings their expertise to bear on the subject, and uses it to help the reader form a judgement.

Research

Some people see reviewing as a soft option. How nice to be given the best seats in the theatre or copies of interesting books, all for free. As soon as you try to write a review you'll realize that it isn't as simple as that.

Example
Before you can review a play, you need to research the playwright. Is it their first play? If not, was their last one a hit or a flop? Is this play another one on a theme they've already explored, or a whole new subject for them? You also need to know about the director, and the leading actors. What's their track record? Why are they doing this play? Then there's the production. Is there anything interesting or unusual about the lighting, scenery, costumes and so on? All of these things have to be researched before you can think about enjoying the play.

All reviews will involve some sort of research, not just the play in the example. You need to have knowledge of both the practitioner and the art form. In the case of restaurants and hotels, you need to know something about the chef or the hotelier before you can assess their product.

Types of review

Reviewing areas include:

▶ *theatre*
▶ *films*
▶ *television*
▶ *music*
▶ *books*
▶ *visual arts*
▶ *restaurants and hotels.*

THEATRE

Readers will inevitably be interested in anyone famous who is involved in a play, but don't forget to give credit to other members of the team if their contribution is outstanding in some way. Be careful to distinguish between the actor and the character they are playing. If you are discussing the character, give the actor's name in brackets afterwards. For example:

> *John Smith gives an indecisive performance as Hamlet* – this criticizes the performance.

> *Hamlet (John Smith) is chronically indecisive* – this describes the character.

The director also plays a major role in any theatrical performance, often it is their stamp on a production which makes it good or bad. If this is a new play have they created something memorable or if it is an established play have they come up with new ideas and do these ideas work?

When reviewing an amateur production for a local paper take into account the difficulties and limitations that amateur companies face. Take your cue from the audience – if they seemed to like it, or were clearly bored, use that as the foundation of the review.

FILMS

In many ways this is like reviewing theatre but you also need
an understanding of the technology involved and the history of
cinema. Again, you are assessing a team effort so pay attention to
the direction, cinematography and so on, as well as the actors.

TELEVISION

TV reviewing covers all types of programme, not just drama, and
the rule about expertise is partially suspended. A reviewer should
understand television but does not need to be an expert in the
subject of, for instance, a documentary. The reviewer is more like
an ordinary viewer, watching TV to be educated and entertained.
This means that TV reviews, unlike other reviews, rarely castigate
programme makers for errors of fact.

MUSIC

Music reviews cover both live performance and recorded music.
With performance consider all the aspects that make for a good
experience, not just the music.

BOOKS

Fiction reviews should not be a retelling of the plot, but rather
an assessment of the work as a whole and its place both in the
writer's body of work and in the current fiction climate. In your
notes, look at all aspects of the book – characters, plot, theme,
writing and so on – but only mention in the review anything that
is particularly well or badly done, or particularly important for
that book.

With non-fiction, a reviewer needs to know what other books on the topic are available and whether the new one is an improvement on them, or fills a niche. If the book has errors of fact this should be mentioned.

VISUAL ARTS

These can be difficult to review because of the need to describe in words something that was designed to be visual. However, many publications will also run a photo of at least one item from an exhibition.

RESTAURANTS AND HOTELS

Restaurant and hotel reviews aim to convey the experience of an ordinary customer. Professional reviewers almost always visit the premises anonymously, and many go to great lengths to make sure that they don't become well known and recognizable. A few of these reviewers are so famous they make no attempt to be anonymous, and their reviews are quite different.

Taking notes

A reviewer first and foremost needs to try to experience the subject of the review in the same way as their readers will. For all sorts of reasons this is difficult – the reviewer won't have spent their own money, they may have the best seats in a theatre or be in a small dark screening room instead of a cinema. The biggest difficulty is the need to record their reactions at the same time as they are having them, and a system for taking notes is essential.

Don't write all the time. Jot down those things that really leap out at you, and only write enough to jog your memory later on when you are writing the review. You should already have amassed the necessary facts during your research, so concentrate on noting your impressions and your emotions. Also make a note of any quotes that you may want to use, whether it's the page number for a book or a line from a play or even a remark by a waitress. (Restaurant reviewers have to develop ways of taking notes without being seen of course and film and theatre critics have to scribble in the dark.) At the end, write one short sentence, or one word, that summarizes your experience.

With book reviews it can be tempting to read the book twice, making notes the second time, but it's the first time that really counts and that's when you should make your notes. Only read the book again if, when you start to write the review, you suspect you're being unfair in some way.

Writing the review

Before you write the review, decide what your overall opinion is. Start with the note you made at the end and decide whether that needs enlarging. You may have written 'brilliant' or 'dreadful', but that isn't enough – maybe it should be 'brilliant but too long' or 'dreadful script but visually beautiful'. Your review will work towards this judgement and be shaped by it.

Next, draw up appropriate questions and answer each one. The questions fall into two categories, factual and judgemental.

Typical factual questions are:

▶ *What is it called?*
▶ *What is it about?*
▶ *What kind of work is it?*
▶ *Who created it?*
▶ *Who appeared in it?*
▶ *Who directed it?*
▶ *Who else was involved?*
▶ *When can it be seen?*
▶ *Where can you buy it?*

- ▶ *When is it set?*
- ▶ *How much does it cost?*

Typical judgemental questions are:

- ▶ *Is it good of its kind?*
- ▶ *Does it add anything to our culture?*
- ▶ *Will my readers engage with it?*
- ▶ *Is there evidence for my opinion?*
- ▶ *Does it achieve its aims?*
- ▶ *Is it technically competent?*
- ▶ *Is it worth the money?*

Not all of the questions will be relevant to every type of review, but you should answer all of those that are. Then decide which are important enough to feature in the review.

As you write the review always keep your reader in mind. Don't imagine the artist (or chef) reading the review and reacting to it. Focus on the questions the reader will be asking: Will I like this? Is it any good? What's it about? and so on.

List the good points and bad points that your notes and questioning have thrown up. Weed out the ones that you are not going to bother with. Don't feel that you have to write about every aspect of the experience, it's better to concentrate on a few important things.

The review will end with your overall judgement, so structure the points to lead up to this. Decide on an order for them, keeping good points and bad points in groups rather than jumping from good to bad and back again.

Don't feel that you have to suspend judgment if you are reviewing local or amateur productions. By all means try to find positive things to say to balance any negative criticisms, but if the public is paying money then the production should provide value for money and if it falls short then this needs to be said.

FACTS

House style will dictate how you present the necessary facts. Some publications put them at the head of the review, some use a fact box. If there is no guidance put them in the second paragraph, after the introduction.

INTRODUCTIONS

As with all journalism, the introduction has to catch the reader's attention. Try to write an introduction that will appeal to someone who doesn't think they are interested in the subject of the review. A provocative quotation, an anecdote or a surprising statement all work well – but if you make it too contentious be prepared for a backlash.

BODY COPY

Work through the points that you have already decided to make, linking them where possible. Where you give an opinion, always explain and give an example:

- ▶ *Don't write 'The plot is full of holes.' This opinion needs explanation and example.*
- ▶ *Write 'The plot is full of holes. When James produces a gun to shoot John, we have no idea how he got hold of it. It looks just like the gun that Jack handed in to the police in Act 1.'*

Insight

If you can't find a concrete example to back up your opinion, then re-examine that opinion and ask yourself if it is valid, otherwise your readership will query your judgement and think you are being biased.

Most reviewers try to avoid revealing surprise endings and plot twists, although sometimes this means you can't write about something important – all you can do is drop hints.

ENDINGS

Sum up your judgement, and add any caveats that you feel
are required. For example: 'This book is a little short on detail,
but it does provide a good basic introduction to the subject.'

LANGUAGE

Use the past tense for things that have happened, such as a meal
in a restaurant, or a one-off concert and for a one-off occurrence,
such as a performance being cancelled or an understudy taking
over. Use the present tense for everything else (including book
reviews).

There is no need to use phrases like 'I think that' or 'In my
opinion'. Also avoid vague adjectives like 'brilliant' and 'dreadful' –
these are fine in your notes but the review needs more concrete
descriptions.

DOUBLE-CHECK

While it is tempting to go off on flights of fancy there is no
room in a review for waffle or purple prose. Take out everything
which is irrelevant and if you are making a statement, check
your facts.

REACTION

Having written your review you must be prepared for a reaction,
particularly if the review was negative. When reviewing local
amateur dramatic productions or books by local writers you will
probably either know the people concerned or you soon will. This
makes it imperative that your review is fair and accurate as you
may have to justify it to them personally.

Previewing areas

These include:

- *product information*
- *market news*
- *forthcoming events*.

PRODUCT INFORMATION

This can be anything from a short paragraph lifted from a press release to a full description or test of a new product. Sometimes products are compared and rated, more like a review than a preview.

MARKET NEWS

Many publications have a market news page which may include product information but which can also include company news that is relevant to the readers and information about possible future developments in the field.

FORTHCOMING EVENTS

Magazines will run previews of relevant events, such as exhibitions, trade fairs and celebrations.

Writing a preview

Most previews are very short and the real skill lies in condensing the information down into the fewest possible words. Product comparisons are longer, and the main requirement is for a means of assessing the products that the reader can understand easily. Give each item marks out of ten, or a number of stars, to show how good, bad or indifferent it is.

Libel

If your review is to be a bad one, you might be concerned that the subject of the review will take action of some sort against you. 'Fair comment' means that you can say anything that is your honest opinion. You mustn't be malicious and you mustn't make it impossible for the person to earn their living. For these reasons you shouldn't write reviews on anything where you have personal issues. Always declare any bias or personal interest in the review.

The subjects of the review are in the public domain and so you are entitled to review them, but it is not kind (and could be thought to be malicious) to give a hostile review to something that was not in fact receiving much publicity and was likely to languish in obscurity without your review.

Always take legal advice if you have any doubts about what you have written.

Exercises
- ▶ *Read reviews of the same thing in several different publications and compare both the reviewers' opinions and the style of the reviews.*
- ▶ *Choose an item to review.*
- ▶ *Make notes for the review.*
- ▶ *Write the review for a specific publication.*

10 THINGS TO REMEMBER

1 *Become an expert in your chosen field.*

2 *Keep your knowledge up to date.*

3 *Research the subject of your review in order to add extra background detail.*

4 *Be passionate but open minded when reviewing.*

5 *When reviewing plays, films, books and so on, don't give the ending away.*

6 *Take plenty of notes.*

7 *Make sure you spell names correctly.*

8 *When making a criticism, back it up with a concrete example.*

9 *Answer the questions you think your readers would ask.*

10 *Pitch your writing to the level of your readership.*

22

'How-to' and other practical articles

In this chapter you will learn:

- *about ways of addressing the reader in a practical article*
- *how to structure a practical article*
- *about illustrations.*

> *What do you look for in a feature article? A unique*
> *viewpoint, a bit of flair, and real experiences.*
>
> Mike and Jane Jago, Editors, *Motorcaravan Motorhome Monthly*

'How-to' articles feature in most magazines. Technical and hobbyist publications will carry the most, but many magazines have recipes or tips. Again, the advice is to concentrate on what you know and analyse the magazine you want to write for to ensure you follow the house style. Analysing the magazine will also tell you what level of expertise you can assume in the readers.

Insight

Be sure you understand the topic thoroughly yourself, but bear in mind that you are writing for people who know much less about it than you do.

First person, second person or imperative?

Which you use will depend on the type of article and the house style. Articles giving advice on how to do something will be written in the second person, simple recipes and other how-to articles will be written in the imperative. For example:

First person:

When I make a Victoria sponge, I always beat the eggs and sugar together first.

Second person:

If you have to change a tyre, it is a good idea to loosen the wheel nuts before jacking up the car.

Imperative:

Turn on the oven to gas mark 5.

Sometimes how-to articles are a mixture of first person and second person where they include directions and explanations. This makes for a friendlier feel to what can be rather dry writing:

You must grease the tin before pouring in the batter, but I always line it with greaseproof paper as well.

Order

The order for a straightforward how-to article will always be sequential, but other articles of a practical nature can start with the most important facts. Whatever you do, make sure that there is an underlying logic to the order.

Start by analysing exactly what you need to tell the reader – break the information down into a series of small items and put them into the most logical order. This will give you an outline for the article.

The piece should start with anything that needs to be done first, such as setting the oven temperature (because it takes time to heat up) or giving a list of items needed for the task:

> *Knitting a blanket square: 1 × 50 gram ball of double knitting wool, a pair of size 8 or 4 mm knitting needles, tape measure.*

Next, define any terms if necessary. This will depend very much on the readership. If the blanket square above is for a knitting magazine, it would be reasonable to assume that readers know the meaning of terms such as 'stocking stitch' or 'k2tog'. On the other hand, if it is part of a series for beginners you may need to explain some terms but not others, depending on what has gone before.

Now write the main body of the piece, working through your outline. If you are describing something very technical try to give the reader breathing space between chunks of information. A summarizing sentence can do this nicely:

> *You should now have 96 squares, each measuring 15 cm × 15 cm. Next we will look at how to join them together into a blanket.*

Once you have drafted the article, if at all possible, give it to someone to read. Ask them if it makes sense, and if they think they could do the task. It is surprisingly difficult to explain things clearly and straightforwardly.

Insight

Always double-check your instructions – a missed step in the process could lead to letters of complaint.

Illustrations

Most how-to articles require illustration of some sort. Recipes are usually accompanied by a photograph of the finished dish, and these are taken by professional food photographers. Some magazines will also include photos of the various stages of preparation. With other types of how-to article, you can take your own photos. Some technical articles will require drawings such as wiring diagrams.

Insight

If you can provide the illustrations for your article you will have a much better chance of placing it. Depending on what you are describing they can be drawings or photos.

Exercise

▶ *Write a how-to article for a task that you are familiar with.*

10 THINGS TO REMEMBER

1 *How-to articles are usually written in the imperative.*

2 *Take account of the expertise level of your readership.*

3 *Write instructions in a logical order.*

4 *Have someone else test your instructions.*

5 *Define terms used if necessary.*

6 *Provide illustrations of photographs if possible.*

7 *Most magazines feature a 'how-to' article of some kind.*

8 *Using summarizing sentences helps break up chunks of technical information.*

9 *Write about what you know.*

10 *Start the article with anything that needs preparing first.*

23

Travel writing

In this chapter you will learn:
- *about the qualities a travel writer needs*
- *about outlets for travel writing*
- *about the practicalities of travel.*

> *Be yourself, don't try to be Bill Bryson...*
>
> Mike and Jane Jago, Editors, *Motorcaravan Motorhome Monthly*

Travel writing is often seen as glamorous and lucrative, a way of being paid to take a holiday. Of course, the truth is that commissions have to be sought just as with any other type of writing – and that when you are working, a holiday isn't really a holiday any more.

Travel writing is also one of the most popular forms of journalism and rejection is frequent. Not all magazines will take copy from freelancers and tourist board press officers won't provide information unless they believe you are a bona fide writer. Because it is an overcrowded market it is more difficult to break into without journalistic qualifications. However, travel writing isn't confined to typing up notes on a coral beach describing the beauties of azure seas and luxury hotels – there are other outlets (see below).

Qualities needed

A travel writer needs the same insatiable curiosity and interest in words as any other journalist plus a few other qualities:

- *a sense of adventure*
- *a love of travel*
- *an independent nature*
- *good health*
- *an abundance of patience.*

Types of travel article

There are two main types of travel writing:

- *writing for travellers*
- *writing for non-travellers.*

In both types of writing you should try to convey the feel of the place, but if you are writing for travellers you'll also need to give hard information about travel arrangements, costings, safety and so on. Writing for non-travellers is more descriptive and anecdotal since its main purpose is to entertain.

Within the two types there are many ways of approaching travel articles including:

- *travel tips, i.e. a travel 'how-to'*
- *round-up, comparing similar experiences such as amusement parks*
- *journey, i.e. the actual travel*
- *adventure*
- *food and drink*
- *special interest.*

Outlets for travel writing

There are specialist travel magazines such as *Wanderlust* and *National Geographic Traveler* magazine which feature nearly all travel writing in one form or another. Most consumer magazines have regular travel or holiday features. Airline magazines are often looking for pieces based on personal experience. Hobbyist magazines will feature travel where it relates to their speciality. For example, a riding holiday in Bangkok might be of interest to a horse magazine, while a trek across the Sahara in a three-wheeler could interest the editor of a car magazine.

Getting started

The tips given in Chapter 2 all apply to travel writing. Write for free, for newsletters or small local publications until you have built up a portfolio and then try to get paid commissions.

> **Insight**
> At the time of writing, e-zines like *Itchy Feet* and *Far Flung* take unsolicited articles. They don't pay, but give useful writing experience and could be usable in your portfolio of cuttings.

If you have already begun to sell features, talk to the editors who know you about their requirements for travel features. Also consider using your specialized knowledge in a way that links with travel.

> **Example**
> A writer who has been selling articles to a specialist needlecraft magazine could offer an article on traditional Portuguese embroidery based on their trip to that country.

Ideas, angles and hooks

Because so many people want to be travel writers, the ones who succeed are those who come up with the best ideas. To get commissioned or have an article accepted you will have to be innovative. Again, start with what you know such as your expertise or hobbies and then look for an unusual travel angle as suggested in the example above.

Starting with what you know can also mean looking at the area where you live in terms of a travel article. Just because it is familiar to you doesn't mean it is familiar to readers in another part of the country or even another part of the world. Keep an eye on any developments in the travel industry. If your local airport increases its destinations, a local magazine might be interested in a feature on one of the more unusual ones.

Remember that linking ideas to dates, events, seasons or people can make them more interesting.

Insight

Don't forget it is essential to have a good hook to pull the reader in. Writing about the most famous buildings in a city has been done many times, but, for example, finding a link between them, such as their architects or building materials will give a new slant.

Getting commissions

Once you have done your initial research, contact editors with ideas for articles. Tell them when you're planning to travel and when you'll be able to deliver the article.

In America, if you are commissioned, the editor will give you 'Letters of Assignment' which you can use to negotiate price reductions on accommodation and so on and which will open doors when it comes to arranging interviews. Letters of Assignment are not given in the UK but on occasions you may be required to show some proof that you are a professional writer. An email from the editor or logging on to the magazine's website showing one of your articles may be sufficient. If you think there may be a problem with obtaining an interview, send a pdf file in advance of your most recent article which has the publication's title, your byline and the date.

Interviews

If you need to interview people for the article try to set this up before leaving. Allow plenty of time for this, because gaining access to officials in some countries can be a lengthy process.

Organizing a trip

Being well organized means that you will make the most of your time during the actual trip. Do plenty of research into the place you are visiting. Ask for press kits from tourist boards and combine these with information from travel guides and the internet. Decide on a focus for the trip and be realistic about how much you can fit in.

DURING THE TRIP

Keep a diary where you make notes of all your experiences and sensory impressions and also make careful note of any facts and figures and spellings of names. Take plenty of photos as a record of your trip even if you don't plan to provide photos with your article.

Writing a travel article

As with all other feature writing you should write in an appropriate way for your target magazine and ask yourself

'What will my reader want to know?' Readers will be asking questions such as:

▶ *What's it like to be there?*
▶ *Can I afford to go there?*
▶ *How hot/cold is it?*
▶ *How safe is it?*

When writing, use action verbs to convey immediacy and cover the five senses (sight, sound, touch, taste and smell) to give the reader a feeling for the experience. Avoid adjectives that make your piece read like a brochure, such as 'wonderful' or 'spectacular'.

Insight

Check and double-check your facts. You may be encouraging your readers to travel halfway around the world at great expense – they don't want to get there and find the attraction they went for has closed.

Photographs

More and more magazines want you to supply photos with copy – in fact, your words may be rejected if you don't supply high quality, professional pictures. Unfortunately they don't pay extra for these.

You'll find that tourist boards, government agencies and chambers of commerce are almost always keen to provide photographs as a way of getting free publicity and encouraging visitors. Editors of travel magazines will also have access to photo libraries. However, some articles will rely on photos taken by the writer and if you are aiming at the top end of the market you will need a top quality camera. And if you are not a competent photographer take a photographic course.

Maps

Some articles may need to be accompanied by a map, but these are usually copyrighted so you will need permission to use them and will probably have to pay. Often the magazine is able to supply these. Alternatively, draw your own sketch map.

Travelling free

Sometimes well-established travel writers are offered press trips and other free jaunts. There is nothing wrong with this, but bear in mind that whoever is paying for the trip will have an agenda. Also some magazines won't take features where there was an element of subsidy in the trip, so check with the editor before accepting the commission.

Practicalities

Finally, learn to travel light and pack like a professional. Unless the trip requires special luggage (such as a rucksack for an adventure holiday) use one suitcase with wheels. Try to take crease-resistant clothes that will mix-and-match and pack them by rolling rather than folding.

Insight

When meeting people on a travel-writing trip you owe it to them and to your magazine to look as smart as possible. For instance, if you hang clothes up in a steamy shower room on arrival, the creases will drop out.

If you are flying, check the hand luggage rules and keep within them. Hand luggage should include your camera and any other equipment such as a tape-recorder. A padded rucksack is good for this – dedicated camera bags are an obvious target for thieves. Also include in your hand luggage a toothbrush, a change of underwear and any medication in case your suitcase goes astray.

Make two photocopies of your passport and any other important documents, such as insurance policies, in case the originals are lost or stolen, and leave one set with a contact at home.

Exercises

▶ *Choose a travel experience of your own and write it up.*
▶ *Illustrate it with: a photo, a drawing or a sketch map.*

10 THINGS TO REMEMBER

1 *Travel writers need a sense of adventure.*

2 *Articles for travellers should include costings and additional relevant information.*

3 *Articles for non-travellers should be entertaining as well as descriptive.*

4 *Build up a portfolio by writing for free for local papers and small publications.*

5 *Buy a good camera and learn how to take good photographs.*

6 *Look for interesting angles to sell your article such as 'Beekeeping in Peru'.*

7 *Do plenty of research in advance of your trip.*

8 *Take plenty of notes including your impressions.*

9 *Include what a place sounds like, smells like and feels like.*

10 *Learn to travel light.*

24

Writing a column

In this chapter you will learn:
- *about the different types of column*
- *about generating ideas for a column*
- *about syndication.*

What do you look for in a feature article? It's got to tell you something you haven't read on the web, in the papers or seen on TV. Great, exclusive pictures are almost as important as the words.

Chris Jones, Editor, *Golf World*

Types of column

Regular columns are a feature of most magazines. The most likely scenario is that a writer will be an established freelancer before they are given the chance to write a column. An editor needs to be very certain that a writer is reliable and can produce consistent quality work before awarding them a regular slot. Most writers are not as fortunate, or as talented, as Jeffrey Barnard, whose long-suffering editor regularly had to run the line 'Jeffrey Barnard is unwell' when the column failed to appear on his desk on time. Types of column include:

▶ *specialist advice*
▶ *celebrity*
▶ *political*

- *sporting*
- *humour*
- *personal*
- *think pieces*
- *agony aunts.*

SPECIALIST ADVICE

Certain specialities are found over and over again in magazines, such as medicine, law, gardening, wine, cooking, DIY, parenting and pets. In addition, specialist magazines will have advice columns relating to their subject area. These columns are often a series of replies to readers' letters, but another common pattern is to have a short (say 500-word) piece by the columnist, followed by two or three letters with answers. If you have specialist knowledge then try offering your services as a columnist.

CELEBRITY

These are often ghost written. Sometimes the celebrity barely knows what is in their column but often the columns are a genuine collaboration between a writer and a well-known figure with plenty to say, but no time to write. The writer should insist on some sort of formal credit. This usually takes the form of the words 'as told to' or 'in conversation with' followed by the writer's name, all in rather small type under the celebrity's name.

POLITICAL

These are usually written either by politicians or by professional journalists, but if politics is your passion then you could approach a magazine. Choose one that is likely to agree with your stance.

SPORTING

Sport is generally considered to be a male interest, although it would be more accurate to say that men are more likely to read about sport than women. Men's magazines do often carry sporting columns, whereas women's magazines rarely do.

HUMOUR

This is a difficult area to break in to and there are very few writers who can produce good quality humorous material regularly. Usually they have made their name in some other area of comedy first.

PERSONAL

A first-person column gives a little slice of the columnist's life. They are often humorous, but don't have to be.

THINK PIECES

These are often, for some reason, the last item in a magazine and are essay-like musings around a topic. They are similar to personal columns in that they are the writer's personal view point and are often a platform for strong opinions that are not necessarily editorial policy.

AGONY AUNTS

Although this usually involves answering readers' problems, the writer will often preface the letter with words of wisdom.

Insight

Columnists are often contentious. One of their roles is to voice the feelings of many of their readers who don't have the opportunity to put their frustrations into words.

Practicalities

IDEAS AND DEADLINES

A column writer's life is an endless series of deadlines. Some writers like to live dangerously, knowing that they do their best work when they leave it until the last minute and write against the deadline. Most prefer to plan ahead.

Whether the column is weekly or monthly it is worth looking a year ahead and planning the obvious landmarks, such as the Christmas column. Then look at that specific year and see if there are any anniversaries that would be relevant to your readers and would make a good column. Some columns, such as gardening, have a seasonal aspect, and for personal columns you can use your own important dates such as birthdays.

Not only can you allocate a few slots this way, but you can start to draft the columns out. Be prepared to be flexible. If something more interesting happens that would fill that slot, then use it, and keep the original draft for another time. You should also have a few general purpose columns written, because you might suddenly have to pull a column – for instance, if you'd written a light-hearted or critical piece about a celebrity who died suddenly. Whatever your subject, make sure you tie it in with something topical and relevant to your readers.

Insight

If you are writing a specialist column, be sure to pitch it at a level appropriate to your readership. This might mean avoiding jargon, specialist terms or arcane references.

STYLE

All column writers require a strong personal style that comes through in their writing. Readers come to know what to expect and look forward to reading the column. Even if the column is about you, try not to use 'I' too many times. Make sure to include plenty of references to outside events and other people – very few of us have the power to keep readers interested in our own inner workings and nothing else.

Always ask yourself what aspect of the column your readers will identify with. If you are too superior and all-knowing they will, at worst, dislike you, and at best feel outclassed by you. A little self-deprecation goes a long way.

Established columnists often have the freedom to give their hobby horses an airing, and columns generally allow for stronger and more one-sided opinions than ordinary journalism. Readers accept that a column is individual and doesn't necessarily reflect editorial policy.

The downside of this is that you are more likely to receive criticism from readers and possibly even abuse. On the whole editors like to see letters coming in – even critical ones – because that shows the column is being read; but you will have to learn to take it on the chin. Your readers will feel that they know you, and will feel free to write comments that they would never say to your face. And they are right – after all, the columnist chooses to put their opinions into the public domain.

Syndication

Some columns are syndicated, that is the same column appears in more than one magazine at the same time. This is more common in America than the UK because it is geographically larger and the magazines won't cover the whole of the country.

Exercises
- ▶ *Make a list of at least 20 ideas for a regular column that you could write. This can be any type of column that you choose.*
- ▶ *Choose one idea and write it up.*

10 THINGS TO REMEMBER

1 *Many columns are written by people with specialist knowledge such as sport.*

2 *Columnists have to be able to stick to deadlines and produce copy regularly.*

3 *Pitch your writing at the level of your readership.*

4 *Plan ahead so that you don't miss important dates.*

5 *Research which important anniversaries are due, such as centennials.*

6 *Develop a personal style.*

7 *Don't use the word 'I' too often, even in a personal piece.*

8 *Be prepared for criticism from readers who don't like your opinions.*

9 *Have some general articles written in advance in case a piece has to be pulled.*

10 *Syndicated columns are more common in the USA than the UK.*

25

Fiction

In this chapter you will learn:
- *about the market for magazine fiction*
- *to analyse stories in magazines*
- *how to submit stories.*

> *Please read* The People's Friend *for several weeks. Try to work out how the authors have achieved what we want. But don't just write a carbon copy of something already published. Try to be original.*
>
> Angela Gilchrist, Editor, *The People's Friend*

Fiction in magazines usually means short stories, although occasionally an excerpt from a novel is used. There is no doubt that the market for short stories in magazines is shrinking. At one time all women's magazines carried one or more stories per issue, but now many of them rarely carry stories, or only carry stories by well-known writers. In addition, a small number of literary magazines take fiction.

However, there are still some outlets, one of the best known being *The People's Friend*, which buys hundreds of short stories a year. There are also small subscription-only magazines which carry nothing but short stories. Sometimes these offer payment by way of prize money (see Appendix B). Added to this, there are several e-zine sites which take short stories for small or no payment. They are mainly American.

Stories in magazines

The best way to get a feel for the type of short story which is popular in magazines is to read as many as possible and then analyse them. Choose a target magazine and read several issues to see what the stories have in common and pitch your writing to match. Count the words in two or three stories to see what the typical length is.

Contact the magazine and ask if they have writer's guidelines specifically for short story writers. Subscription-only magazines often have their guidelines on their website. Be prepared to be told that the editor is overwhelmed with submissions and isn't looking for any more stories. As a general rule, womens' magazine stories are between 2,000 and 4,000 words long, have a female central character and a happy ending. The story needs a strong emotional line.

Stories fall into two main categories – either the reader will identify strongly with the central character or the reader will fantasize about the character. So, for example, a story about a single mother could explore her feelings of loneliness and end with her meeting a new partner. If the single mother is an ordinary woman with a part-time job in a supermarket then the reader will identify with her, but if she is a model flying all over the world, with a full-time nanny and a jet-set lifestyle then the reader will fantasize.

Stories online

There is a strong market, particularly on American e-zines for mystery and horror stories as well as other genres. Some welcome 'flash fiction' (stories of fewer than 1,000 words and even as few as 50). Although there will be little or no payment, these sites make a good starting point for honing your skills and providing what people want to read (see Appendix B).

COMPETITIONS

Some magazines run regular short story competitions with publication as the prize. It is important to read previous prize-winning stories to get a feel for what is wanted.

Writing the story

Short story writing is a challenging and specialized form of fiction. If you are deeply interested in it, then study it as a separate topic, but here are some important points that will help:

▶ **Have one central character, and be clear in your own mind who this is.** *The focus of the story must stay with that character, and the ending should bring resolution to that character's story.*

▶ **Don't choose a plot that would need a novel to explain.** *Short story writers have to use great discipline in the construction of their plots.*

▶ **Have a strong narrative thread.** *The easiest way to do this is to give your central character a problem at the start of the story that is resolved at the end.*

▶ **Don't have a predictable ending, look for a twist or a surprise.** *However, this should make sense within the context of the story.*

These are guidelines not rules, and many good short stories have not followed them, or at least not followed every single one of them. With fiction, unlike journalism, it is very important to find your individual voice as a writer and so style can often be more significant than content.

Some fiction writers spend a lot of time planning their story, others plunge straight in and start writing, letting the story take them where it will. Whichever way you do it, once you have a reasonable draft put the story away for a while and come back to it fresh.

Presentation

Unless the guidelines say they accept email submissions, send a hard copy. The stories should be typed or printed on A4 paper, on one side only, leaving a wider margin on the left-hand side and double-spaced. As with all magazine writing, keep the layout simple, don't use fancy fonts and make sure you do a spellcheck.

Submissions

Unlike articles, short stories should be written out in full and sent on spec. A proposal won't tell an editor how well you can write, which is more important in short stories than the idea.

Include a covering letter and if relevant your CV. If you want your story returned include a stamped, addressed envelope (SAE). If your story has a seasonal content or is tied in to a specific date or anniversary make sure you submit it at least six months before.

Exercise
▶ *Choose a magazine or an e-zine and write a short story for it. Submit it if you wish.*

10 THINGS TO REMEMBER

1 *Read several copies of the magazine you wish to write for to check the type of fiction they publish.*

2 *Look for subscription magazines as they often use more short stories than mainstream magazines.*

3 *Ask for the magazine's guidelines and stick to them.*

4 *Have only one main protagonist in a short story.*

5 *Don't have more than one subplot – many short stories don't have any subplots.*

6 *Ensure your story has a strong narrative thread.*

7 *Be prepared to write several drafts to create a polished piece.*

8 *The first paragraph must be intriguing enough to persuade the reader to continue with the story.*

9 *Number the pages and put the title and your contact details at the bottom of each page.*

10 *Write your story in full before sending it off.*

Part four

Developing a career

26

The next level

In this chapter you will learn:
- *about becoming more professional*
- *about networking*
- *how to manage contact information.*

> *Before you write an article, find out if anyone wants to buy it! Phone features editors of relevant magazines and put the idea to them. If they are interested they will almost always suggest angles that would suit their publication, though it's an even better idea to suggest an angle (preferably unusual!). If no one is interested at least you've saved yourself the trouble of writing something no one wants.*
>
> Tim Rumball, Editor, *Amateur Gardening*

Once you start to taste success then it is time to move up a gear and become more professional in your approach. This is especially important if you don't want to run out of ideas for future articles, or magazines in which to place them. So now is the time to start thinking about:

- ▶ *membership of professional bodies*
- ▶ *subscribing to professional magazines or websites*
- ▶ *networking*
- ▶ *managing information*
- ▶ *having your own personal website.*

Membership of professional bodies

There are several professional bodies which cater for the freelance writer. Probably the best known is the National Union of Journalists which as well as offering advice and support to its members also publishes a *Freelance Directory*, which is now available online. Details of other writer's organizations are given in Appendix B.

Subscribing to professional magazines and websites

This serves two purposes. It:

▶ *keeps a finger on the pulse*
▶ *provides a way of networking by putting your profile on the relevant sites.*

In the fast moving media world it is essential to keep abreast of what is going on, where the commissions might come from and who is working where.

MAGAZINES

The *Press Gazette* is probably the best known one. It keeps its readers abreast with what is going on in the media world, but also has a page where freelance writers can advertise.

WEBSITES

There are various websites which offer directory facilities to writers – some are free and some are a subscription service. Once you are listed you'll find that PR companies start sending you press releases relevant to the subjects you write about.

Networking

Even if you only intend to write part-time, networking can make a huge difference. Making contacts and building good relationships could lead to more commissions or leads*. Whenever you use one of your contacts, remember to thank them and always send them a copy of the article.

Insight

Networking is an important way of finding out where the writing opportunities are, what editors are looking for and creating good relationships. Always carry plenty of business cards – you don't want to run out just as you meet someone who could be useful.

Editors are only human and if they are looking for someone to commission they will want to work with a writer that they already know. Needless to say that writer also has to produce the goods, on time and in the required format.

People skills have been dealt with in Chapter 10 but there is also a practical side to networking and this involves:

▶ *making contacts*
▶ *providing business cards*
▶ *follow-ups.*

MAKING CONTACTS

This involves actively trying to meet and get to know people who are in the magazine world. You will probably have to try a variety of ways of doing this because good contacts can come from unexpected places.

---

*Lead: the initial contact that turns into an article.

It is not easy starting from scratch, but by now you will already know a few editors, so build on this. Take up any work that's offered in the early days and make yourself useful whenever you can. Never turn down a social invitation where you might meet other editors or writers.

Sign up for writing courses or join writing groups which specialize in journalism. Take up invitations to press launches even if you are not interested in the product or subject. This way you will get to know other freelance journalists and photographers.

Having met new people, make sure you remember their names. There are various techniques for doing this:

▶ *Try to make a connection between their name and something about them, such as what they do or what they look like.*
▶ *When first introduced, try to use their name as often as possible in the conversation to fix it firmly in your mind.*
▶ *As soon as you can, write down new names in a notebook or electronic organizer. Also include useful information about them.*

Keep an updated list of editors of all the magazines you have either already contributed to, or wish to contribute to. If they move to a new magazine, try to keep in touch because if they have used your work in the past, they may want to again in their new magazine. Don't assume that they will keep your contact details.

Keep abreast of staff changes by checking the relevant magazine. Otherwise check the publication's website if they have one. But be aware that information on the website doesn't always get updated. To be on the safe side, ring up and ask the switchboard.

BUSINESS CARDS

If you want people to remember you and your details, you will need to have business cards to hand out. These should have your phone numbers (landline and mobile), email address and website if you have one.

If you work from an office then put that address on, if you work from home you may prefer to keep that private. Consider having a PO box number if you don't want to give your home address. These are not expensive, and mail can be collected from your nearest sorting office or, for a higher fee, delivered to your home.

You can have your cards professionally printed either by your local printer or through websites which offer a competitive service. With the new technology professional printing is not as expensive as it used to be. Or you can design and print them on your computer, but if you decide to do this aim for a professional look. Scruffy, amateur-looking cards will not enhance your reputation. The money spent on having your own business cards will pay off in the long run and they are a tax-deductible expense.

As well as handing out your own cards collect as many business cards as you can from other people. You never know when their knowledge or expertise will be useful to you, so file them in a suitable container with an index so that you can quickly find the one you want.

Of course, it is possible to exchange business cards via Blackberry and no doubt future technology will make physical cards redundant.

Insight

When designing your business card, leave the back blank. When you're networking use them instead of scraps of paper – that way every time you give someone helpful information you also give them your contact details.

FOLLOW-UPS

When you have made contact with an editor or someone else who may be helpful to you, try to keep in touch so that they don't forget you. This is not going to be a one-sided relationship, so be prepared to be helpful to them.

Once a magazine has accepted an article the editor will probably be prepared to listen to further proposals. However, there is a fine line between harassing them with endless ideas and subtly ensuring that they know you are capable of providing more articles.

Managing information

Keep close at hand useful names and phone numbers, including:

▶ *magazines and their editors*
▶ *local and national newspapers*
▶ *libraries and record offices*
▶ *people who have information or expertise.*

INDEXING

If you are trying to make money from writing you won't want to waste precious time looking for information so a comprehensive indexing system – whether on paper or the computer – is essential. It is also essential to keep it up to date.

STORING REFERENCE INFORMATION

Information which has been downloaded from the internet can be stored on your computer, but to ensure you know where to find it again you will need to set up a filing system with an index and the name of the folder that the piece of information is stored under. Ensure you put in each folder the name of the website and the name of the person who owns the copyright to it.

If the information could be useful for more than one article either cross-reference it or put copies in each article's file.

Having acquired all this information, make sure you don't lose it again. Put in place a regular back-up regime so that important information is not only stored on your hard drive but also on CD, memory stick (sometimes called a flash drive) and store it somewhere safe, away from the computer. If you computer crashes, is damaged or stolen you will be able to recover most of your records.

It is possible to have two hard drives on your computer and save information on both as a back-up, but it is more useful to have portable back-ups because they can be used on another computer if yours has crashed.

There are also internet companies which, for a fee, will store information on their computers. Some also offer a recovery service if you have accidentally deleted an important file. See Appendix B.

Personal website

Even if you subscribe to commercial websites it is still useful to have your own website. Your internet service provider may give you a free site, but this will probably be limited in scope. Otherwise you can launch your website on one of the free providers or a paid one.

Your site will need a domain name and registering it will stop anyone else using it. Nominet is the internet registry for all domain names in the UK. While it is possible to register your domain name directly with them, it is easier and probably cheaper to use one of the registrar agents. The Nominet website has a list of them and it pays to check out the differences in the prices they charge for registering and the services they offer.

These sites will also tell you if your chosen name has already been registered as well as offering facilities for hosting your website. If you chosen name has been registered, for example, as www.myname.com it may still be possible to register it as www.myname.co.uk or www.myname.net or with any of the other endings available (see Appendix B).

Professional website designers will give a site a slick look, but it is perfectly possible to design your own website, using one of the software packages available for the task. Don't be too ambitious and aim for a clean simple look.

Your home page should be welcoming, with links to all the main parts of the site. Web pages are not like pages in a book or magazine in that they contain much less information. Each page should only have enough information to fill one screen and there should be plenty of space between groups of text to make it easier to read. Although known as white space it can be any colour background.

As for content, your site needs to be entertaining as well as informative. Say something about yourself, give samples of your work and make it lively and interesting or people won't linger. Remember web surfers don't like to scroll, they like to click, so have a lot of pages with links between them.

Insight
Once your website is up and running, establish plenty of links with other sites. This means that browsers will find you and it also means that you are more likely to show up on search engines.

10 THINGS TO REMEMBER

1 *Join a professional body which will give you advice and support.*

2 *Subscribe to professional magazines and websites to keep abreast of the current situation and opportunities.*

3 *Create your own website as a shop window for your skills.*

4 *Network as much as possible to get yourself known.*

5 *Always carry business cards to hand out.*

6 *Keep up to date with changes to magazine editors.*

7 *Keep a comprehensive contacts book.*

8 *Make good relationships with editors even if they are not taking articles from you at the moment.*

9 *Set up a good indexing system so that you can find information quickly.*

10 *Set up a regular back-up regime so that important information is not lost.*

27

Writing as a business

In this chapter you will learn:
- *about writing full time*
- *about legal obligations*
- *about business practicalities.*

> *The most common mistake writers make is not bothering to keep up to date with the proposed target market. 'Market research' might be dirty words to some, but is essential.*
>
> Suzanne Ruthven, Editor, *The New Writer*

If you have begun to have some success as a features writer you may be tempted to make it a full-time job. There are two ways of making a full-time career out of writing:

▶ *working for a magazine as an employee*
▶ *working for yourself as a full-time freelance writer.*

Training

Whichever you choose, consider taking a journalism course, or look for a job on a local publication where you can learn the business even if you ultimately intend to be freelance. The National Council for the Training of Journalists (NCTJ) is probably the best known provider of journalistic qualifications.

It offers a range of courses which include both full-time courses at accredited centres around the country as well as home learning and short courses to upgrade skills. To test your skills try out the test (self-test information) in the distance learning section on their website.

The Periodicals Training Council (PTC), which is part of the Periodical Publishers Association (PPA), gives guidance and training for careers in magazine journalism. PPA members can take the PPA Professional Certificate in Journalism which is useful for people working in the industry who have no formal qualifications.

The London College of Communication (formerly the London College of Printing) offers a range of courses in journalism.

Websites for the above are listed in Appendix B.

Going it alone

If you decide to become a full-time freelance writer you will need to consider the emotional impact of changing from a part-time hobby to earning a living from writing. While there are plenty of advantages to being a freelance writer – not least being your own boss – there can be downsides and these include:

▶ *motivation*
▶ *financial security*
▶ *negotiating payments and expenses*
▶ *chasing unpaid invoices*
▶ *health*
▶ *tedious jobs.*

MOTIVATION

Unless you are lucky enough to get sufficient commissions from editors you will have to come up with ideas and constantly send out proposals until a commission comes through. Provided you give editors what they want then this should get easier but in the meantime it is a question of sticking at it and not losing heart. If things go quiet you will have to put extra effort into getting commissions, so if you are someone who easily loses motivation then freelancing may not be for you.

After good writing skills, perseverance and determination are the main qualities needed for success as a full time freelancer. Decide on the number of proposals you need to send out a week to make a living and stick to that target.

FINANCIAL SECURITY

Not everyone likes the excitement of being responsible for their own financial fate. Will you be able to sleep at night when times are hard? Will you be able to say no to commissions when you are overstretched?

Insight

To earn a living as a freelancer it is not only necessary to have lots of ideas and editors waiting for your copy, but you must have a business plan and keep control of your finances.

NEGOTIATING PAYMENTS AND EXPENSES

While many magazines will pay the standard industry rate others might be open to negotiation. There is also the question of who pays your expenses for a particular article as well as negotiations for the kill fee. If you find it embarrassing to talk about money, then negotiating will be tough for you.

CHASING UNPAID INVOICES

Many of us find it difficult to chase people for money owed to us, but it is a fact of life when you are running your own business and it has to be done.

HEALTH

There is no sick pay for freelance workers, so you need good health, or at least the ability to keep working through bouts of bad health.

TEDIOUS JOBS

There will always be a tendency for editors to offer a freelancer the work that no one on the staff wants to undertake. In the early days you will have to be prepared to accept this cheerfully.

Obligatory matters

If you have decided that writing is going to become more than just providing the odd article in magazines or newspapers, you will need to put things on a business-like footing. There are various factors to take into account starting with legal obligations.

INCOME TAX, NATIONAL INSURANCE (NI) AND VALUE ADDED TAX (VAT)

HM Revenue & Customs (HMRC), which was formed in 2005, following the merger of Inland Revenue and HM Customs and Excise Departments, is now the body responsible for collecting Income Tax, NI contributions and VAT. Everyone setting up their own business needs to register with them as self-employed, either as soon as they start or within the first three months of starting. Failure to do so could result in a fine. Information on how to register can be found on their website along with other useful information. See Appendix B on useful websites.

Everyone has a basic annual tax-free allowance and when their income goes over that amount then they have to pay tax. With NI, all income is liable but people with very low earnings can apply for a Small Earnings Exception. However, you won't have to pay VAT until the annual taxable turnover on your self-employed income exceeds the much higher VAT threshold, which at the time of writing is £64,000.

You will have to complete a tax return in respect of your earnings from writing, even if you are also employed and pay tax through the PAYE system. If you file your tax return online then all the sums are done for you automatically. However, you do have to key in the correct information. If this seems daunting, then you will need to employ an accountant – their fees can be set against tax. Whichever way you do it, you need to keep all receipts relating to the business.

Income from journalism can be very variable and the Inland Revenue allows writers and journalists to balance out their tax liability between good years and bad years. This is called 'averaging' and it is fully explained in leaflet IR234.

Other matters

Further considerations include:

- ▶ *state benefits*
- ▶ *pensions*
- ▶ *insurance*
- ▶ *using the home for business.*

STATE BENEFITS

Many state benefits are means tested (in other words, if your income goes up, your benefit goes down, or is cancelled altogether). The rules are very complex and vary from benefit to benefit. The Citizens Advice Bureau can give advice on this, so check their website or seek advice from the NUJ if you are a member.

PENSIONS

Your National Insurance contributions are used to fund your state pension, but you also should consider making extra pension provision. Employees usually have the benefit of a company scheme with employer's contributions as well as their own, but freelancers have to entirely fund their own pension. Take professional advice.

INSURANCE

You will need to consider various types of insurance including:

► *car*
► *buildings and contents*
► *public liability*
► *loss of earnings.*

Car insurance: Most car owners are only insured for private use, and if you use your car to go to interview people or visit somewhere in connection with your writing this becomes a business use and your insurers should be told. Your rates will probably increase.

Buildings and contents insurance: You should tell your insurers that you are using your home for business. If you have invested in expensive office equipment it ought to be insured.

Public liability insurance: You may be covered through your buildings and contents policy, but check with your insurers to make sure you are covered in the course of your business as well as private activities. If you are not, it would be prudent to remedy this.

Loss of earnings: If you are relying on your writing income to cover all the bills then consider insuring against loss of earnings if you become incapacitated.

USING THE HOME FOR BUSINESS

Most writers work from home rather than running to the expense of buying or renting office space. However, if you are working from home, you should first check with your mortgage company or landlord, if you are in rented accommodation, to ensure there are no restrictions on use. If you have to make any structural alterations check with the planning office at your local council to see if you require planning permission. Check with your local valuation office to see whether you will have to pay business rates on the rooms you are using. Finally, if people are coming to your home, do a risk assessment to ensure you comply with Health and Safety regulations.

Practicalities

There are practical considerations to take into account. These include:

- ▶ *having a business plan*
- ▶ *cash flow*
- ▶ *work space*
- ▶ *equipment*
- ▶ *record keeping*
- ▶ *invoicing.*

BUSINESS PLAN

Even if a plan is not required for bank loan purposes it is worthwhile spending time and thought on how you propose to make the business work. On a practical level you need to work out how much income you require, how much time you can spend on writing and whether you can seriously generate the amount of work needed to pay the bills. Then decide how you are going to promote your business, and finally write down your long-term goals and where you want to be in one year's time or five years' time or ten years' time.

The high street banks and some other financial institutions give small business advice, but bear in mind that they will be looking to increase their own business. The Government has set up an organization called Business Link which provides essential small business advice, and young writers can get advice from the Prince's Trust. Both have websites (see Appendix B).

CASH FLOW

In most businesses there is a gap between providing a product and receiving payment and freelance writing is no different – it could be several weeks or even months between writing an article and getting paid for it. In the meantime, if writing is your only source of income, you will need to ensure you have sufficient money or overdraft facilities to pay your way.

Fortunately, unlike many other businesses, writing does not have huge start-up costs, nor does it incur high expenses which have to paid up front.

WORK SPACE

While it is possible to dash off a few articles on a laptop balanced on the corner of the kitchen table, this is not practicable for running a business. A writer who is planning to earn their living freelancing will need space for equipment, filing cabinets and book shelves. It is possible to utilize the corner of a room or even a large cupboard; the key point is to get it organized.

Shelves and a filing cabinet will be needed for reference books and documents in current use to make them easy to access. They don't have to be expensive or elaborate. Planks on bricks will hold books just as well as oak bookcases, and cardboard boxes can act as filing cabinets. If space is at a premium, reference material that you only need now and again can be packed in storage boxes and put in the attic or under the bed. But don't forget to label on the outside what is in each box or you will spend hours tipping them all out. Also make a full list of the contents of the box and put that inside, at the top.

EQUIPMENT

A computer and printer are a must once writing becomes more than a hobby. Whether you use a laptop or a standard PC it should be on a proper desk or table at the right height for correct typing, otherwise you will find yourself suffering from aches and pains. A broadband connection is also necessary, not only because emailing is becoming increasingly important, but because so much research can be carried out on the internet where download speed is of the essence.

At the time of writing, a photocopier, phone message service, a tape-recorder and a digital camera are all essential. Fax machines are not as essential as they once were, but on occasions they may be the only way of receiving information from someone who doesn't have access to a computer or a digital camera. However, as we move into an increasingly technological age, with faster access to information through hand-held devices, like Blackberries, while on the move, these could all become obsolete.

RECORD KEEPING

It does not matter whether records are done with pen and paper or on the computer, what is important is that they are kept up to date and properly indexed. Keep records of your income and expenses. This is essential for tax purposes and is better done on a regular basis to keep on top of it rather than leaving a pile of invoices and receipts to be looked at once a year. If your earnings run to it, using an accountant saves time and should save money.

Also keep full records about articles. This is so that you can keep track of the various ideas and commissions you have out in the market place. Note the following:

▶ *the name of the idea or article*
▶ *the date it was sent out*
▶ *whether it was by email or post*
▶ *the name of the publication and the editor*
▶ *any photographs attached*
▶ *acceptance or rejection.*

Insight

A good filing system pays dividends in saved time and effort. Whether your information is stored on your computer, or as hard copy, file in under appropriate headings and cross reference where necessary.

INVOICING

Like any other business you are selling a product and you will have to invoice the magazine which purchases your article. Again, this is better done sooner rather than later because some magazines might only pay invoices once a month. Include the invoice with the article so that the editor can pass it straight on to the accounts department.

Design a simple invoice template that includes the following information:

▶ *your name*
▶ *your contact details*
▶ *a space for the name of the article*
▶ *a space for the name of the publication*
▶ *your fee*
▶ *your expenses*
▶ *the total payable*
▶ *VAT if applicable.*

Give each invoice a unique number, but don't start numbering from 001 as this shows you have only sold one article, start from an odd number such as 049. And be sure to keep copies of all invoices.

Insight

Be sure to take regular computer back-ups. Have a regime in place to back up current work at the end of each day, and your whole system at the end of each week. Don't keep the back-ups in the same room as the computer.

10 THINGS TO REMEMBER

1 *Don't rely on freelancing for a full-time income unless you have the skills and motivation to persevere.*

2 *Be prepared to negotiate your fees and chase unpaid invoices.*

3 *Make sure you comply with all legal obligations such as Income Tax, National Insurance and VAT.*

4 *Check with your landlord or mortgage provider that you can use your home to run your business.*

5 *Make sure you have a viable business plan, particularly if you want a loan or overdraft facilities.*

6 *Ensure you have enough money to cover the gap between an article going out and the money coming in.*

7 *Ensure you have sufficient space to accommodate a computer, printer, filling cabinets and book shelves.*

8 *Put in place a comprehensive filing system.*

9 *Either include an invoice with your article or get in the habit of invoicing regularly.*

10 *Set up an accounting system so that you know what your expenses are and what monies are outstanding.*

28

Starting your own magazine

In this chapter you will learn:
- *about starting a magazine*
- *about the need for advertising*
- *about production and distribution.*

The most important question is whether or not there is a market for your publication – and that means it needs to be attractive to advertisers as well as to readers. As an editor your main preoccupation is bound to be about the quality of editorial content.

But without advertising income you will not have a sustainable product. So once you have set your editorial goals, it's important that these are shared as widely as possible with potential advertisers and sponsors.

Design and print quality are equally important and it's worth taking time to select the right people to work with. Then all you have to do is make sure your distribution system works – so that you can prove you have a readership. Shifting even a few thousand magazines is hard work, as is selling advertising to people who get bombarded with requests!

The best way to win them over is through your readers so distribution is crucial. Some advertisers will demand

editorial content; be wary of that unless you are simply
producing an ad magazine. It's also important these days to
think about the content of your website. We have actually
launched our own internet TV channel.

Then take note of feedback and make adjustments if
necessary, both in content and distribution, but be aware
that it will take time for any new publication to become
established and you will need to have confidence in your
own product to make it work and to win advertisers over.

When reader reaction starts to build – and advertisers start
phoning you – you can allow yourself a glimmer of pride
and satisfaction. On publication day one of my former
editors would hold up the first copy off the press and
proclaim 'another minor miracle'. Then it was back to work
to start preparing the next one. Once it's in the blood there's
no greater thrill.

Steve Egginton, Mendip Times, Mendip TV

If you are not having much success in getting editors to take your
articles, but you are confident about your writing abilities, then, as
you can see from the above quote, another alternative is to start a
magazine of your own. It is difficult, but do-able as many writers
have proved.

All the points which were highlighted in Chapter 27 on writing as
a business will have to be taken into account and it is even more
important to have a good business plan and to ensure you have
your cash flow covered because the set-up costs will be higher and
the gap between having to pay out for services and receiving an
income will be longer.

There are various options:

- *conventional magazines*
- *e-zines and fanzines*
- *franchise.*

Conventional magazines

The traditional paper magazine is still the most popular format and if you decide to go down that route then you will have to do some market research and check the following:

- ▶ *gaps in the market*
- ▶ *potential readership*
- ▶ *how to make it distinctive*
- ▶ *selling points.*

GAPS IN THE MARKET

Whatever type of magazine you have in mind, the first thing is to check out all the other magazines covering the same field and assess whether there are any gaps in their coverage. If, for example, you are interested in producing a sports magazine and all the other sports magazines are national ones, there may be a slot for a local magazine which can give more space to all the local sports that probably don't get a mention in the nationwide publications.

POTENTIAL READERSHIP

For a magazine to be successful you need to be clear who you are aiming it at – this includes age, gender and social level. In the above example, clearly the readership will be anyone interested in sport, particularly at a local level – but will they buy it? This can only be tested by doing some market research and asking people.

Insight

Encourage feedback from your readers. This way you will know whether the magazine is reaching your target readership and whether you are providing the kind of magazine they want. Having got the feedback, make the necessary adjustments.

HOW TO MAKE IT DISTINCTIVE

In the above example the fact that there will be much more coverage of local sporting events will make the magazine stand out from its competitors – other kinds of magazines will need to have their own distinctive slant.

SELLING POINTS

Readers will buy a magazine if it provides the kind of information they want. With a sports magazine, printing all the results could prove a good selling point. Another way is to include plenty of names and faces because most people like to see themselves mentioned in print. There are some readers who buy a magazine because they're looking for a specific product and want to check out the adverts.

The next considerations are:

▶ *advertising*
▶ *cover charge*
▶ *subscription*
▶ *free*
▶ *coverage*
▶ *number of publications a year*
▶ *size*
▶ *number of pages*
▶ *quality*
▶ *distribution*
▶ *printers, publishers and typesetting.*

ADVERTISING

It may seem strange to make this the first consideration, but unless you can fund the project yourself, it will be necessary to sell advertising space to cover most if not all of the production costs.

The price of adverts will depend on how much you estimate it will cost to produce the magazine, plus something to give you an income. However, businesses who buy advertising space expect value for money and there will be plenty of competition for their revenue so it is essential to get the prices right – charge too much and no one will advertise, charge too little and you won't cover your costs. Check out what other similar magazines are charging for adverts and use that as a base figure. Ideally you should aim to be cheaper.

However, the cost of advertising space is not the only consideration, advertisers will only advertise in publications which produce results for their products and they will need to know that the magazine is reaching the right kind of readership and being read.

Allied to this is deciding the ratio of advertising to editorial. As said in Chapter 3 this varies from magazine to magazine, but it is a crucial to get this right for your magazine because if there are too many adverts people won't read it and if there are too few you won't cover your costs.

Persuading businesses to take adverts (known as selling space) is hard work. If you do not have an aptitude for selling then you will need to find someone who has and they will need paying. You could offer them a percentage of the fees charged on all the space they sell.

COVER CHARGE

Most magazines are paid for by the reader at the point of sale. If the cover charge is set high enough to cover all production costs then the magazine will be too expensive and won't sell, so the cover charge is pitched to compare well with the competition and advertising revenue makes up the shortfall.

SUBSCRIPTION

Some magazines are sold by subscription only, others are available in the shops as well as by subscription. The advantages of subscription are: knowing how many copies to print and the lower distribution costs. Many specialist or hobby magazines are subscription only for this reason.

FREE

Many locally-based magazines cover all their costs from advertising and are given away free.

COVERAGE

This can be:

- ▶ *national*
- ▶ *county-wide*
- ▶ *local.*

National: While it might seem ambitious to plan a magazine which will have national distribution, if you can find a niche in the market which does not have its own specific magazine it could be a viable option.

County-wide: Most counties, or special geographical areas, have glossy monthly magazines, but it is worth checking out this market to see whether there is scope for another one.

Local: Local magazines could offer the most scope for the writer who wants to start their own. Look at the existing local service and see if you can find a niche.

NUMBER OF PUBLICATIONS A YEAR

This will depend on several factors including how much advertising can realistically be sold, how much material it will take to fill the pages and the type of magazine. Women's magazines tend to be weekly, fortnightly or monthly. County and local magazines are mostly monthly. Specialist magazines are often bi-monthly (every other month) or quarterly and a few are yearly.

SIZE

When you look along a newsagent's shelves it is easy to see that the most popular size for magazines is around A4 size – some are slightly larger. This gives attractive-looking pages with space for around a 1,000-word article and perhaps a couple of photographs.

A5 size is a popular size for local publications, or anything which has to be posted. However, the actual size will be dictated by the type of magazine and how much it is going to cost to print. Printing is cheaper if you use a standard size.

NUMBER OF PAGES

Magazine pages are calculated in fours because they are printed on both sides of large sheets. So the number of pages will be four, eight, twelve and so on, and you will always have to manipulate your material to fit.

QUALITY

This includes:

▶ *type of paper*
▶ *colour or black and white.*

Types of paper
There are two kinds of magazine paper:

▶ *coated: this is the glossy paper most used for most magazines*
▶ *bond: cheaper than glossy and usually used for A5 local magazines, news letters, booklets and so on. It comes in different thicknesses which are measured in grams. Most magazines are produced on bond paper ranging from 80 to 130 grams.*

Colour or black and white
Full colour (sometimes called four-colour) is expensive but most readers expect it, particularly for glossies. Even magazines printed

on bond paper are now usually printed in full colour. Possible exceptions are specialist or hobbyist magazines.

DISTRIBUTION

There are four options available.

- ▶ **Sold through newsagents:** *Usually newsagents take magazines through their wholesaler, who don't deal with individuals, so you would have to work through a specialist company (see below).*
- ▶ **Posted:** *Subscription magazines are usually sent through the post so this has to be factored into the costs.*
- ▶ **Hand-delivered:** *This is usually for free magazines covering a relatively small area and, unless you plan to deliver them all yourself, you will have to pay someone to do it.*
- ▶ **Left at distribution points:** *Again this is for free magazines and is the easiest and most cost-effective way of distributing them. However, to ensure the magazines get read, you must choose distribution points that are easily accessible and will be visited by those interested in your magazine. For example, a magazine on local facilities for school children could be distributed via local schools if they are willing.*

PRINTERS, PUBLISHERS AND TYPESETTING

There are plenty of small printers around who can print magazines. A starting place would be to see who prints other magazines in your area. There are also companies which will handle everything for you from selling the advertising space to distributing the copies. Of course, there is a charge for this and they will only take you on if they think your magazine is viable. You can choose how many of their services to use.

Insight

Building a successful magazine takes time. If you have done your market research and are confident that you are filling a gap in the market, have confidence in your product and build it up slowly.

E-zines and fanzines

With more and more people using the internet, these could offer a cheap way of producing your own magazine. It is possible to start with a simple blog* or a newsletter and expand it to become a multi-paged magazine. However, e-zines are in their infancy and most people still want to hold a magazine in their hands to read it.

Again, look for a niche market or a local angle to attract sufficient hits. This is important when it comes to selling advertising space, which you will need to do to generate an income. The other way of making money is to have most of the site set up for subscription payers only.

> **Insight**
> Have a website alongside the e-zine so that you can promote it.

If you have a passion for one particular activity or celebrity you could start a fanzine, either paper or electronic, and reach out to other people who share your interest. Fanzines are rarely profit making and you may not even cover your costs.

Franchises

There are opportunities to buy a franchise of an existing magazine. These are usually locally-based A5 magazines covering geographic areas. The advantages are you should be given plenty of back-up and training from the franchise holder and you will be buying into a proven market.

If you decide to start your own magazine from scratch and your idea can be expanded to other areas in the country then there is nothing to stop you selling franchises.

*blog: online diary

Desktop publishing

Printing small-scale magazines on your own computer could be a way of testing the market before you launch a full-scale magazine.

It is possible to create simple magazines using the software which has come with your computer, such as Microsoft Publisher. However, for more sophisticated layouts use a specialist software package. There are plenty to choose from and some of them are free to download. Others can be bought new and second-hand from Amazon.

10 THINGS TO REMEMBER

1 *Do your research to assess where there is a gap in the market.*

2 *Clarify your readership and provide the kind of information they are looking for.*

3 *Have a good business plan in place.*

4 *Try to make your magazine distinctive.*

5 *Establish how your magazine will be funded, either by advertising alone or advertising plus cover price.*

6 *Employ someone who is good at selling advertising space as that is where the bulk of your income will come from.*

7 *Set the price of advertising space at a competitive rate.*

8 *Make sure the income from the magazine is in excess of production costs.*

9 *Decide how your magazine will be distributed to the public.*

10 *Try to get reader feedback to pass on to advertisers.*

Appendix A: Submission guidelines

Most magazines produce guidelines for writers, some very short and some long and detailed. Below we have given edited highlights from a few of them, but always ask your target magazine for their guidelines and check the editor's name in case they've changed.

The Oldie magazine

(courtesy of *The Oldie* magazine)

Polite notice: It will help you if you have read at least one issue of *The Oldie*, so that you get a feel for the kind of thing we publish.

SUBMITTING ARTICLES FOR CONSIDERATION

We are happy to consider unsolicited articles on any subject.

We do not commission articles from ideas or treatments, only from assessing finished work. Articles should be between 600 and 1,000 words in length, typed, double-spaced, and accompanied by a SAE. Please send to Jeremy Lewis, Features Editor, *The Oldie*, 65 Newman Street, London W1T 3EG.

Please do not send unsolicited articles by fax or email. Response will be in writing, and usually takes two to three weeks.

We are particularly interested in unsolicited pieces for our 'I Once Met' and 'Olden Life' slots, although well-written articles on any subject are always welcome. We do occasionally publish short stories, although not more than two or three a year. If photographs or illustrations accompany your piece, please send copies and not originals. We will contact you if we need to use originals for reproduction purposes. *The Oldie* cannot be held responsible for the loss or damage of any unsolicited materials.

Please note that we do not accept poetry.

A WORD ABOUT EMAIL

Please try to avoid sending correspondence as attached files – typing or copying and pasting directly into the email is the best way of ensuring that we receive what you send.

Please remember to include your full name and address on your emails.

The Scots Magazine

(courtesy of *The Scots Magazine*)

EDITORIAL GUIDELINES

The Scots Magazine has a team of regular professional contributors, but is also keen to encourage the submission of material from all writers and photographers. The following notes provide some basic guidelines.

GENERAL

We are a publication concerned with specifically Scottish topics. There is a minimum of four months between acceptance and publication: please take this into account if an article is aimed at a particular issue. It is not unusual for material to remain in stock for up to two years before publication.

Manuscripts should be typed, using double-spacing, with a substantial margin, and only on one side of the paper. The first page should start half-way down to allow for typesetting instructions.

Any relevant photographs, drawings, maps, diagrams, etc. should be enclosed with the text, and each item must bear the contributor's name and that of the copyright holder if different. Each illustration should also carry a brief caption explaining its significance in the article. Writers receive proofs to check, prior to the publication of articles. We prefer articles with a word-count of around 1,000–2,500 words, but these limits are not rigid. We do not buy material that has already been published elsewhere. A SAE with submissions is appreciated.

It should be borne in mind that this page is not a plea for material, rather a collection of hints on how to improve the chances of success. *The Scots Magazine*'s acceptance rate of speculative submissions is less than 5% – but you could be in that number.

GETTING THE FLAVOUR

Before writing for any publication it is essential to know the type of material it uses. By reading *The Scots Magazine* every month you will absorb our style and become familiar with the type of topics we deal with. As a bonus, you won't need to buy one if you're successful, for we send a complimentary copy of the issue with your article in it. Use the Subscriptions coupon in the magazine to have a copy sent to you for 12 months.

PAYMENT

Articles are paid on acceptance. Illustrations, however, are paid on publication as the number we can use is not known until the page make-up has been completed.

COPYRIGHT

The Scots Magazine buys first copyright only, so that once we have printed your material you are free to offer it for publication elsewhere. When submitting photographs and other illustrations whose copyright is not held by the sender, it is incumbent on the contributor to obtain permission for their possible use in *The Scots Magazine*.

PHOTOGRAPHS

We can cope with all sizes and formats, but for colour we prefer original transparencies of 35mm and upwards. All material is returned to photographers after publication. Please enclose a suitable SAE for this purpose. Digital images must be high resolution pictures. (Our Photography Guidelines contain more information.)

EDITING

Don't worry about spelling or grammar if you think you have an article worth writing, for all material is thoroughly sub-edited before publication. In the course of preparation, even professional texts have to be reduced or altered and you should not expect your author's proofs to be word for word with your manuscript. You may also be asked to elaborate on certain passages or add new paragraphs.

PRELIMINARY APPROACH

If you wish guidance on any aspect of contributing, *The Scots Magazine* staff will be pleased to help you. Write to us at – *The Scots Magazine*, D.C. Thomson & Co Ltd, 2 Albert Square, Dundee DD1 9QJ.

Email: mail@scotsmagazine.com

---

easyJet Inflight magazine

(courtesy of Ink Publishing)

FEATURES

Each issue of *easyJet Inflight* contains between six and nine main features, each of which must be based in or around easyJet destinations and be of interest to the wide range of easyJet customers.

We are interested in stories that sell the easyJet 'experience' and by that we mean independent foreign travel.

THE AIRLINE AND MAGAZINE'S BRAND VALUES ARE:

Optimistic – friendly, welcoming, approachable, forward looking, innovative.

Irreverent – humorous, witty, spontaneous, independent in spirit.

Provocative – bold, outspoken, enthusiastic, sense of adventure, challenging.

Simple – what you see is what you get, functional, unpretentious, classless, nothing to hide.

We don't generally accept straight travelogues or first person pieces, unless the writer is an expert or high profile. Given that we want to impart an on-the-ground 'insider's knowledge' feel, we prefer features from those who either live in, or are very familiar, with a destination rather than travel writers who visit for a few days.

Think along the lines of specific events that are noteworthy (Tour de France), very unusual activities (Etna volcano tours) or unusual hooks (Trabant Tours of Berlin) as recent examples of features that have worked very well.

easyJet Inflight's tone is chatty, irreverent, light-hearted, innovative and fun. Academic and hard-news styles should be avoided. Stories should not be overly promotional, but independent.

Most *easyJet Inflight* features range from 1,000 to 1,400 words, depending on the subject. Subheads work well, as do information box-outs.

Compensation varies depending on the type of feature and is competitive with other magazines.

PROPERTY

We have a dedicated property feature every month, and are interested in articles that move beyond providing basic property information.

BUSINESS

Our business section features light business features, which should conform to the general tone of the publication.

HOW TO PITCH EASYJET INFLIGHT

Most of the features are written by freelancers, although please note: we do not accept unsolicited manuscripts. If you are interested in writing for *easyJet Inflight*, please send ideas only, not completed features. We do commission writers we have not used before, but only those whose published clips demonstrate a high proficiency in magazine writing.

We prefer pitches to be made by email as opposed to telephone. We do not accept pitches which aim to promote specific products or businesses.

Please look through recent issues of *easyJet Inflight* on our website (www.easyjetinflight.com) to research our style and to make sure we have not recently run a piece on the topic you are proposing.

Writers must include credentials, and published clippings.

Prospective contributors doing preliminary research for a story must avoid giving the impression that they are representing *easyJet Inflight* or INK publishing. They may use the name of the magazine only if they have a definite assignment. We expect writers to be objective and adhere to journalistic codes of ethics. easyjet.ed@ink.publishing.com

The People's Friend

(courtesy of *The People's Friend*)

The '*Friend*' is the famous story magazine, so obviously we place a lot of importance on that. We buy hundreds of short stories every year.

Then there are our serials – we run two at a time, because the readers enjoy a continued story so much. Story series don't appear regularly, but are always extremely popular when they do.

Before you start... please study the market.

So please, read *The People's Friend* for several weeks. Then, try to work out how the authors have achieved what we want.

But don't just write a carbon copy of something already published. Try to be original.

COMPLETE STORIES

These vary in length – between 1,000 and 4,000 words usually. Deeper, more emotional, stories tend to need more space than lighter ones. We also accept short, short stories, from 500 to 1,000 words, for our occasional complete-on-a-page fiction.

We're always looking for good Christmas stories (as well as other seasonal material) but beware the well-worn themes! Again the message is – be original and try to reflect the real spirit of Christmas.

We rarely use stories from the viewpoint of animals or inanimate objects. Historical short stories are difficult – it's not easy to be convincing in under 4,000 words. And anything with a supernatural theme tends to get the thumbs down from our very responsive readers.

We strongly suggest you try writing short stories before you attempt our other formats.

FICTION SERIES

These might be considered a sort of hybrid, a cross between a short story and a serial. They are usually based on a strong, central character in an interesting situation.

CHILDREN'S STORIES

These are traditional stories for children of nursery and primary age. Somewhere between 500 and 700 words.

FEATURES

These range from short, first-person experiences with a couple of pictures, to extensive photofeatures about a whole area, attraction or event.

FILLER FEATURES

They are usually about 1,000 words long. We're looking for bright, lively articles, full of human interest, on a broad range of topics.

POETRY

Short lyric verse should rhyme and scan as naturally as possible.

SERIALS

These are normally worked on from the early stages by the author and at least one member of staff. All our serials have a strong emotional situation as their central theme, usually family based.

Writing a serial isn't like writing a novel. You have to enthral the reader in such a way that she – or he – is looking forward eagerly to next week's instalment. You don't have the luxury of writing long, beautifully crafted narrative or descriptive passages.

Serials run from 10 to 15 instalments on average, though we will use shorter, or longer, stories from time to time.

The opening instalment is usually quite long – 6,000–7,000 words. Succeeding instalments are shorter, around 5,000 words.

Each instalment is made up of three or four chapters. (Get the idea of differentiating between a chapter and an instalment.)

Each chapter should deal with a particular aspect, or incident, or scene in the story, moving it forward at a good pace.

Your final chapter to the instalment should have a more powerful curtain, so the reader is impatient to know what will happen next.

We very rarely buy a complete serial in manuscript form. Don't even try a first instalment on your own!

Send us your idea, with perhaps just a few pages of the story, and give us a detailed synopsis of how the story develops... and we'll get back to you.

SUBMITTING A MANUSCRIPT

Ten golden rules:

▶ *We're always happy to consider unsolicited manuscripts, but once you've completed your story, try to read it objectively – we know it won't be easy, because you're so close to it and you've obviously put a lot of effort into it. But do try, and ask yourself 'Is this really a "Friend" story?' And answer honestly, now! If the answer is a definite No, please don't send it in. But if you feel it's along the right lines, by all means let us see it. We're here to help and advise you.*
▶ *Your manuscripts should be typed – on one side of the paper only. Use double-line spacing and leave a generous left-hand margin. ALWAYS KEEP A COPY.*

- ▶ *You should also have a flysheet, showing the title and author's name (or pen-name if you prefer). Please make sure your own name and address also appear on the page.*
- ▶ *Number the pages of your story – or serial instalment.*
- ▶ *Staple or clip your manuscript once. And preferably use an A4 size envelope so that you don't have to fold the typescript over. Anything you can do to make your work easy to read will be much appreciated by our hard-working staff.*
- ▶ *Address your short stories to the Fiction Editor at the address below. Children's stories should be sent to the Children's Page Editor and poetry to the Poetry Editor and so on.*
- ▶ *Seasonal stories or articles should be submitted fully three months in advance.*
- ▶ *Remember to enclose a suitable stamped addressed envelope. Or if you live abroad, send an International Reply Coupon.*
- ▶ *Please don't swamp us with manuscripts! We very often find that a collection of stories all have the same basic flaw. So, if you've been enthusiastically writing, pick the best one – or two – to send in to test the water. It'll save your postage – and we'll let you know if we want to see more of your work.*
- ▶ *Be prepared to wait a few weeks for a reply. Our selection process can take some time.*

Payment is on acceptance. You won't have to wait for publication.

The People's Friend
D.C. Thomson & Co Ltd
80 Kingsway East
Dundee, DD8 8SL
01382 462276

Appendix B: Useful websites

Chapter 1: Practical basics

SOFTWARE FOR WRITERS

www.writersupercenter.com – software for managing information.

www.whizfolders.com – software for managing information.

www.azamit.com – software for recording telephone calls.

SHORTHAND COURSES

www.t-script.co.uk

easyscript.com

www.speedwriting.co.uk

www.maegis.com

Chapter 2: Making a start

ONLINE MAGAZINES

www.Helium.com – an American e-zine which offers paid opportunities for writers. There is also the opportunity to evaluate other writers' work. Also runs competitions.

www.bellaonline.com – an American e-zine written by women. No payment but gives writers a chance to see their work online.

www.blogit.com – an American site which promises payment for articles.

www.suite101.com – a Canadian e-zine which offers a share of revenue while your article is on the site.

www.morewriting.co.uk – a British site which gives writers a chance to upload their articles. Also has regular competitions.

www.itchyfeetmagazine.com – a bi-monthly e-zine which takes articles but doesn't pay.

www.farflung.com – an e-zine which takes articles but doesn't pay.

www.hackwriters.com – an American e-zine. Takes articles but doesn't pay.

www.faithwriters.com – Christian freelance opportunities.

www.rd.com/submitjoke.do – an American website for *Readers' Digest*.

www.readersdigest.co.uk – a UK site for *Readers' Digest*. To submit work email excerpts@readersdigest.co.uk or write to The *Reader's Digest* Association, 11 Westferry Circus, Canary Wharf, London, E14 4HE. Mark your envelope with the appropriate department or feature.

Chapter 4: Researching magazines

RESOURCE SITES

www.jbwb.co.uk/markets.html – a British site which gives information on dozens of markets for placing articles, competitions and agents. The site also offers a critique and editing service for all forms of writing.

www.nrs.co.uk – a site for checking magazine readership numbers.

www.firstwriter.com – launched by UK writer Paul Dyson, this is a UK resource site covering literary agents, book publishers, writing competitions, and magazines, from all over the English-speaking world. Users can specify the kind of information they want and receive it in seconds. They can also receive daily InstantAlert emails tailored to their requirements. The online magazine, *firstwriter magazine*, accepts contributions and the site also hosts an annual poetry and short story competition.

www.infoxone.com – a site for checking newspaper readership numbers.

www.bauer.co.uk – gives information on content of several popular magazines.

www.pressgazette.co.uk – press industry subscription magazine.

www.magforum.com – full of useful information regarding magazines and where to find out further information.

PUBLISHERS

www.magforum.com – a resource site listing dozens of magazine publishers.

www.ipcmedia.com – publishes more than 80 of the most popular magazines.

www.pro-talk.com – a business-to-business publisher.

www.imagine.publishing.co.uk – publishes magazines about computers and their accessories.

www.redwoodgroup.net – publishes in-house magazines.

www.inkpublishing.co.uk – publishes customer and consumer magazines and in-flight magazines.

www.archantdialogue.co.uk – publishes magazines.

www.emap.com – publishes 50 lifestyle and specialist consumer magazines.

www.bbcmagazines.com – publishes more than 45 magazines relating to BBC programmes.

www.atompublishing.co.uk – publishes magazines.

MAGAZINES WHICH TAKE ARTICLES

www.parkpublications.co.uk – publishes UK magazine *Country Tales*, four times a year in A5 format and paid for by subscription. Takes articles up to 1,500 words that have a rural theme.

www.chapman-pub.co.uk – a Scottish magazine printed three times a year. Interested in new writers.

www.mslexia.co.uk – a magazine for women published quarterly.

www.family-tree.co.uk – published monthly, takes articles, but has a backlog.

www.theoldie.co.uk – published monthly.

Chapter 5: Ideas

projectbritain.com – contains lots of information on calendar dates, folk lore, customs and so on.

Chapter 8: Considering commissions

www.alcs.co.uk – the Authors' Licensing and Collecting Society is able to remunerate authors with secondary royalties via collective licensing schemes from photocopying and so on.

Chapter 9: Researching information

www.academicindex.net – research website.

historynews.chadwyck.com – an American site for researching old copies of the *Times*. Subscription required.

www.thegoodwebguide.co.uk – independent reviews of the best sites online for food, travel, parenting, money, gardening, wine, property, health, beauty, genealogy.

splunt.com – directory of UK websites.

www.cbdresearch.com – directory site, has to be paid for.

www.opsi.gov.uk – resource site which includes information on the Freedom of Information Act.

www.bl.uk – British Library site which includes newspaper archives.

www.pastpaper.com – supplies back issues of newspapers.

www.whsmith.co.uk – can supply back copies of most newspapers up to nine months' old.

www.eastriding.gov.uk/libraries-archives-and-culture – cuttings agency.

www.ipcb.co.uk – cuttings agency.

www.thepresscuttingagency.co.uk – cuttings agency.

www.highbeam.com – an American site which holds copies of several popular magazines such as *National Geographic*.

www.bbc.co.uk/heritage – has archive information on broadcasting.

www.guinessworldrecords.com – information on world records.

Chapter 11: Organizing the article

www.explorewriting.co.uk – guidance on writing for publication.

Chapter 12: Basic writing skills

www.uefap.com/writing – useful information on grammar.

www.buzzin.net/english – useful information on grammar.

www.studygs.net/wrtstr6.htm – useful information on transitional words.

www.phon.ucl.ac.uk – useful information on grammar.

dictionary.reference.com – an American site which includes a dictionary and thesaurus.

Chapter 13: More about writing

www.editorsoftware.com – useful software for checking to see if your writing conforms to good writing standards. Easy to install and use.

Chapter 18: Illustrations

FINDING AGENCY PHOTOS

www.istockphoto.com – American site which provides photos for a fee.

www.freeimages.co.uk – UK site which provides free photos.

www.bapla.org.uk – UK site which lists photo agencies.

FINDING A PHOTOGRAPHER

www.bipp.com – information on professional photographers.

www.rps.org – information on professional photographers.

PRINTING DIGITAL PICTURES

www.photobox.co.uk

www.snapfish.co.uk

www.bonusprint.co.uk

uk.foto.com

Chapter 23: Travel writing

www.nationalgeographic.com – an American magazine paid for by subscription and published eight times a year by the National Geographic Society. It looks at proposals for articles and pays if it uses them.

www.wanderlust.co.uk – a subscription magazine dedicated to travel writing.

www.bravenewtraveler.com – a Canadian e-zine which is interested in proposals.

www.itchyfeetmagazine.com – a bi-monthly e-zine which takes articles but doesn't pay.

www.farflung.com – an e-zine which takes articles but doesn't pay.

www.hackwriters.com – an American e-zine. Takes articles but doesn't pay.

Chapter 25: Fiction

PRINTED MAGAZINES

www.jbwb.co.uk/markets.html – a British site which gives information on dozens of markets which publish short stories. Also includes information on competitions and agents as well as providing critique and editing service for all forms of writing.

www.chapman-pub.co.uk – a Scottish magazine printed three times a year. Interested in new writers.

www.parkpublications.co.uk – publishes two UK magazines, *Scribble* and *Country Tales*, which are printed four times a year in A5 format and paid for by subscription. Writers can win prize money for their short stories.

www.thenewwriter.com – a British magazine which publishes six issues a year, paid for by subscription. Short stories welcomed but from subscribers and prize winners only.

www.wordsmag.com – a British magazine which has a printed version and an e-zine version, both of which come out four times a year. Payment is by subscription and all profits go to charity. Writers can win prize money for their short stories.

E-ZINES

www.bewilderingstories.com – an American weekly e-zine, no payment.

www.unreality.net – an American e-zine which is printed twice yearly and available by subscription. It pays a small amount for mystical short stories.

www.mytholog.com – an American e-zine paid for by subscription, which pays a small amount for short stories with a mythological content.

www.everydayfiction.com – an American e-zine which is updated daily. It pays one dollar and only takes stories between 50 and 1,000 words.

www.themysteryplace.com – an American bi-monthly e-zine that accepts short stories.

RESOURCE SITES

www.firstwriter.com – monthly magazine paid for by subscription, includes database for writers including magazines, competitions, agents.

www.writewords.org.uk – a British database site offering feedback to writers, support, advice, opportunities, competitions and news. Subscription required.

www.theshortstory.org.uk – information about writing short stories and competitions.

Chapter 26: The next level

PROFESSIONAL BODIES

www.nuj.org.uk – trade union for journalists in UK and Ireland, gives information on pay and conditions, legal advice, membership benefits and training.

www.bajunion.org.uk – the website of the British Association of Journalists.

www.ppa.co.uk – Periodical Publishers Association.

www.cioj.co.uk – The Chartered Institute of Journalists.

www.newspapersoc.org.uk – gives information on all the UK newspapers.

www.nwu.org – trade union for journalists in America.

MAGAZINES FOR JOURNALISTS

www.pressgazette.co.uk – press industry subscription magazine.

WEBSITES FOR JOURNALISTS

www.ifreelance.com – job opportunities for freelancers. Writers can also post their profiles on the site.

www.guru.com – an American website which puts employers in touch with freelance writers. Writers can either pay a subscription to have their names put on the database or pay a proportion of any income generated through the site.

www.journalismuk.co.uk – answers some of the questions new writers like to ask and also has a freelance directory.

www.journalism.co.uk – opportunity to advertise on their freelance page and also has a good directory of other relevant sites.

www.writewords.org.uk – a UK writers' community site. Subscription to access information and to upload work for members' assessment.

www.alcs.co.uk – the Authors' Licensing and Collecting Society is able to remunerate authors with secondary royalties via collective licensing schemes from photocopying etc.

www.plr.uk.com – Public Lending Right is administered by Public Lending Right based in Stockton-upon-Tees and funded by the Department of Culture, Media and Sport (DCMS).

www.societyofauthors.org – the Society of Authors is a trade union for professional authors, dealing with financial and legal problems which they might encounter.

www.ppa.co.uk – the Periodicals Training Council (PCT) oversees the delivery of high quality vocational training for the industry.

www.ppa.co.uk – the Periodical Publishers Association (PPA).

www.writersservices.com – gives details of useful websites for writers in America, Canada, Australia, New Zealand, Wales and Ireland.

OPPORTUNITIES

www.freelanceuk.com – puts freelance writers and potential markets together.

www.people4business.com – puts freelance writers and potential markets together.

www.freelancers.net – features job opportunities.

www.freelancersintheuk.co.uk – comprehensive list of freelancers, including writers, editors, proofreaders and journalists.

www.monster.co.uk – features job opportunities.

www.recruitmedia.co.uk – recruitment site offering freelance positions.

www.allwriting.net – puts writers in touch with job opportunities.

www.ifreelance.com – job opportunities for freelancers. Writers can also post their profiles on the site.

www.guru.com – an American website which puts employers in touch with freelance writers. Writers can either pay a subscription to have their names put on the database or pay a proportion of any income generated through the site.

www.writethismoment.com – a resource site, which includes job opportunities. Although there is an annual subscription fee of £20 or £8 for three months, some of its useful information is available free.

www.writersmarket.co.uk – a resource site, including information on article writing, publishers and competitions. Subscription only.

BACK-UP AND DATA SAVING SERVICES

www.backupdirect.net

www.datafort.co.uk

www.securstore.com

www.thinkingsafe.com

www.adept-telecom.co.uk

www.databarracks.com

www.pro-net.co.uk

www.storegate.com

CREATING A WEBSITE

www.nominet.org.uk – the organization which registers all the domain names in the UK. It also has a list of all the companies which can register names.

www.arin.net – the organization which registers all the domain names in the USA.

www.internic.net – site for regulating the use of domain names and settling disputes, also has list of registered companies which provide domains.

www.123-reg.co.uk – site for registering names and checking whether names are still available.

www.freeparking.co.uk – site for registering names and checking whether names are still available.

www.networksolutions.com – an American site for registering names and checking whether names are still available.

www.allaboutyourownwebsite.com – useful site with information on creating a website.

www.doyourownsite.co.uk – site for creating a website with 30-day free trial.

www.blogger.com – site for writing blogs.

Chapter 27: Writing as a business

TRAINING AND COURSES

www.ca.courses-careers.com – gives information on various ways to get qualified.

www.nctj.com – gives training to journalists, reporters and photographers for the UK newspaper industry.

www.ppa.co.uk – Periodical Publishers Association website.

www.writersbureaucourse.com – tutored home-study course helps you get published.

www.writingschool.co.uk – the Writing School at Oxford Open Learning provides home study and tutor support.

www.journalism.co.uk – freelance journalism courses.

www.yourcreativefuture.org.uk – information on training.

www.train4publishing.co.uk – training provider for book and journal publishers in the UK. Offers short courses on publishing.

www.highbury.ac.uk – training courses.

www.lcc.arts.ac.uk – official site of the London College of Communication; provides information on its courses and how to apply. Includes details for full-time students and life-long learning.

www.lsj.org – provides journalism correspondence courses and writing lessons by distance learning worldwide, and post-graduate diploma courses at the London School of Journalism.

www.doctorjob.com.my – graduate jobs and careers advice, courses and community.

www.learndirect.co.uk – courses.

www.icslearn.co.uk – with details of over 200 courses.

www.uptospeedjournalism.com – training courses in journalism.

www.asne.org – information on training and jobs in America.

www2.ku.edu/~acejmc – accredits and lists journalism courses in America.

ESSENTIAL SITES

www.businesslink.gov.uk – essential information for setting up a business.

www.hmrc.gov.uk – the site for registering Income Tax, National Insurance (NI) and Value Added Tax (VAT).

www.citizensadvice.org.uk – help and advice on legal and money matters.

www.startups.co.uk – advice on starting a new business.

www.princes-trust.org.uk – help for young people starting in business.

www.mybusinessrates.gov.uk – business rates.

www.direct.gov.uk – a site which includes information and advice on pensions, benefits and taxes.

RESOURCE SITES

www.freelanceuk.com – a resource site for freelancers. It carries a wealth of information on starting out as a freelancer, understanding legal and tax issues, tips on marketing yourself, managing cash flow and understanding technology if you work from home, as well as covering routes into the industry, selling your work and useful links to trade associations. There is no subscription fee and at the time of writing journalists could add themselves to the directory for free.

www.gofreelance.com – connects freelance writers with job opportunities.

www.freelancewritersdatabase.co.uk – connects freelance writers with job opportunities.

www.eurofreelancer.com – connects freelance writers with job opportunities.

www.people4business.com – connects freelance writers with job opportunities.

Chapter 28: Starting your own magazine

BLOGS

www.blogger.com – a site for uploading blogs onto.

www.thoughts.com – a site for uploading blogs onto.

PUBLISHING SERVICES

www.writersweekly.com – information on various aspects of self-publishing.

www.warnersgroup.co.uk – offers the complete package of publishing, printing, distributing, selling advertising space, providing editorial.

www.whealassociates.com – offers help with writing, publishing etc.

www.thehardygroup.co.uk – offers help with writing, publishing etc.

www.redactive.co.uk – offers the complete package of publishing, printing, distributing, selling advertising space, providing editorial.

ONLINE PUBLISHERS

www.presspublisher.com – this site gives information on publishing e-zines, payment required.

www.bulletinbuilder.com – this site gives information on publishing e-zines, payment required.

www.formatpixel.com – an online application for creating e-zines, payment required.

FRANCHISES

www.startups.co.uk – site includes tips on starting a business, buying a business and franchises.

www.thegrapevine.co.uk – sells franchises.

www.communitytimes.co.uk – sells franchises.

www.kidsdirect.org.uk – sells franchises.

www.mymaguk.com – sells franchises.

www.getraring2go.co.uk – sells franchises.

www.thefranchisemagazine.net – gives details of various franchises.

DESKTOP PUBLISHING

www.freeserifsoftware.com – free desktop publishing software.

www.5star-shareware.com – for shareware and free downloads.

www.amazon.co.uk – for new and second-hand desktop publishing software.

Appendix C: Glossary

aperture The opening in front of the camera lens that lets the light in when the picture is taken, which is measured in f-stops. A larger aperture has a lower f-number. If you are reasonably close to the subject then a large aperture will make the subject the main focus of the picture.

back-up A copy of work on a computer which can be accessed if the original is lost. Back-ups can be stored both on another part of the computer's hard disk or, more usefully, on a separate piece of hardware or on the internet.

blog Online diary.

brand extension Selling to the readership under the magazine's name items such as furniture and holidays.

brief An editor's requirements for an article.

byline A reporter's name on an article.

catchline Unique word or phrase to identify an article.

cold calling Phoning, or visiting a person or organization that you have not previously dealt with.

copy Written material, the words that make up the article.

cover charge The price paid by the reader.

FASR First American Serial Rights.

FBSR First British Serial Rights.

feature Another word for an article. Includes everything the reader will see on the page, such as pictures or tables.

folio Page.

ghost writing A writer produces work that goes out under another person's name, usually a celebrity.

hard copy Anything printed or written on paper.

in-house Work that is done within a company rather than being sent to outside specialists.

ISBN International Standard Book Number. A unique number by which any book can be identified.

ISSN International Standard Serial Number. It can usually be found on the contents page, along with the volume number and the issue number.

lead The initial contact that turns into an article.

Leader An article in a prominent position at the front of a magazine, often written by the editor.

lead time The time allowed to produce a magazine.

NCTJ National Council for the Training of Journalists.

on spec Sending an already written article without being commissioned.

par Paragraph, word used by editors in a hurry.

piece Article.

pixel Short for 'picture element'. Pictures are made up from thousands of dots of colour. As a rule of thumb, the more pixels there are to the inch, the better the quality of the picture.

....

proofs Roughly printed pages that are checked for spelling, layout, facts etc. before the final version is printed.

....

proposal Suggestion for an article.

....

shutter speed The amount of time the shutter opens to allow the photograph to be taken.

....

staffer Journalist employed as part of the permanent staff.

....

synonym A word that means the same as another word.

....

tabloid Used to describe the style of populist journalism used in the tabloid newspapers (which are half the size of the broadsheet newspapers). In fact, the broadsheets are beginning to change to tabloid size, but the term remains in use.

....

think piece An expression of the writer's opinion, not necessarily reflecting the magazine policy.

Appendix D: Further reading

GENERAL

Atchity, K. *A Writer's Time, Making the Time to Write*
(W. W. Norton, 1995)

Hennessy, B. *Writing Feature Articles* (Focal Press, 1997)

Hicks, W. Adams, S. and Gilbert, H. *Writing For Journalists*
(Routledge, 1991)

Mckay, J. *The Magazines Handbook* (Routledge, Taylor and
Francis Group, 2000)

Saunders, J. *Writing Step By Step* (Allison & Busby, 1989)

Turner, B. (editor) *The Writers' Handbook* (Pan McMillan)

Wells, G. *The Craft of Writing Articles* (Allison & Busby, 1990)

Writers' and Artists' Yearbook (A&C Black)

LANGUAGE

Fieldhouse, H. *Everyman's Good English Guide* (J. M. Dent, 1982)

Gowers, E., Greenbaum, S. and Whitcut, J. *The Complete Plain
Words* (HMSO, 2004)

Hicks, W. *English for Journalists* (Routledge, 1998)

Partridge, E. *Usage and Abusage* (Book Club Associates, 1980)

Room, A. *Dictionary of Confusibles* (Routledge & Kegan Paul, 1979)

The Oxford Manual Of Style (Oxford University Press)

RESEARCH

Hoffman, A. *Research for Writers* (A & C Black, 2003)

LAW

Welsh, T. and Greenwood, W. *Mcnae's Essential Law for
Journalists* (LexisNexis Butterworths, 2004)

TRAVEL WRITING

Dial, C. *Get Your Travel Writing Published* (Hodder Education,
2010)

Index

Page numbers in **bold** type are for glossary definitions

ghost writers, *228, 262, 332*
grammar, *111*
guidelines *see* writer's guidelines
Gunning Fog Index, *133*

hard copy, *179–80, 332*
health, writer's, *287*
home, working from, *289–90*
hooks, *45, 211, 255–6*
Horse + Pony article, *197–210*
hotel reviews, *239*
house styles, *28, 311*
'how-to' articles, *22, 247–51*
human interest, *45*
humour, *22, 141, 263*
hyperbole, *167*

ideas, *38–47, 198, 211, 254–5,*
  263–4, 319
idiom, *111*
illustrations, *36, 67, 183–96,*
  203, 216, 250
image manipulation, *189*
imperative, *248*
indexing, *280*
information management, *280–1*
  see also factual
    information; product
    information; research
information overload, *170*
insurance, *289*
internet, *4, 74–5*
  see also computers; e-zines;
    electronic; websites
interviews, *21, 84–96, 200,*
  212, 227–32, 256
introductions, *242*
  see also opening paragraphs

invoices, *286, 293*
irony, *141*

jargon, *127*
journalism, training in,
  284–5
journalistic writing, *123–36*

key sentences, *172*
kill fees, *69*

language *see* body language;
  vocabulary; writing style
lateral thinking, *42–3*
layout, *179–81, 269*
legal obligations, *287–8*
length, word/sentence, *124–5,*
  129–30, 170–2
  see also size, of magazines
letters pages, *13*
libel, *245*
libraries, *75–6, 184*
link phrases, *215–16*
  see also bridging
    paragraphs
listening skills, *92–4*
litotes, *167*
local newsletters/papers, *11, 78*
look, *165*

magazine business, *17*
magazine content, *20–3*
magazine personnel, *23–4*
magazines, *11–12, 26–37, 78,*
  268, 295–305, 316–17
  for journalists, *276, 324*
main body, *149–63, 153–60,*
  174, 214, 242